INFO-KIDS

How to use nonfiction to turn reluctant readers into enthusiastic learners

Ron Jobe / Mary Dayton-Sakari

Pembroke Publishers Limited

© **2002 Pembroke Publishers**
538 Hood Road
Markham, Ontario, Canada L3R 3K9
www.pembrokepublishers.com

Distributed in the U.S. by Stenhouse Publishers
477 Congress Street
Portland, ME 04101
www.stenhouse.com

All rights reserved.
No part of this publication may be reproduced in any form or by any means
electronic or mechanical, including photocopy, recording, or any information,
storage or retrieval system, without permission in writing from the publisher.

We acknowledge the financial support of the Government of Canada through
the Book Publishing Industry Development Program (BPIDP) for our publishing activities.

National Library of Canada Cataloguing in Publication Data

Jobe, Ron
    Info-kids : how to use nonfiction to turn reluctant readers into enthusiastic
learners

Includes bibliographical references.
ISBN 1-55138-143-5

    1. Reading (Elementary) 2. Children—Books and reading.
I. Sakari, Mary Dayton, 1941- II. Title.

LB1573.J578 2002   372.4   C2001-904113-6

Editor: Jennifer Drope
Cover Design: John Zehethofer
Cover Photo: Ajay Photographics, Photo Disk
Typesetting: JayTee Graphics

Printed and bound in Canada
9 8 7 6 5 4 3 2 1

Table of Contents

Acknowledgments

The writing of this, our second book together, has been a process of discovery. Writing at a distance has had its challenges, but quiet moments on early morning B.C. Ferry cruises between Tsawwassen and Swartz Bay offered time for reflection and insight.

This book has taken a long time in the gestation phase, due to circumstances beyond our control, but it allowed us to have the same talented editor we had for *Reluctant Readers,* Jennifer Drope. Beyond receiving her approval of the manuscript, we are most grateful for her precise and insightful awareness of the intent of our book, and her thoughts for strengthening its structure. We also want to express our appreciation to our publisher Mary Macchiusi for her long lasting patience and encouragement in challenging us in new directions.

We consider ourselves fortunate to be able to have an outstanding children's bookstore to consult: Vancouver KidsBooks. Thanks to Phyllis Simon, who critiqued the manuscript and gave countless suggestions for references, as well as to staff members: Kelly MacKinnon, Christianne Hayward, Sarah Butler and Jonah Hister. We would also like to express our appreciation to the many friends and colleagues who have shared ideas and resources with us and given us such positive encouragement. We are most appreciative of the encouragement and active support of special friends: Jo-Anne Naslund, John Naslund, Margot Filipenko and Matt Filipenko. And, to Paula Hart, for offering so much at both the beginning and the end of the process.

In particular, we would like to thank a host of teachers who shared stories of Info-Kids in their classes, strategies that made a difference with them, and resources that were effective. These include: Bonnie Alguire, Diane Barrie, Erin Boyle, Janice Clark, Russell Collins, Renata de Souza, Barb Dean, Chris Evans, Margot Filipenko, April Gill, Leah Gillespie, Marg Haines, Rennie Hapton, Donnie Henderson, Randi Hermans, Cathie Johnson, Sandy Johnston, Margaret Jorgensen, Sharon Leask, Liz Kloepper, Russ MacMath, Margaret McIntyre, Keith McPherson, Pat Miller, C. Moroney, Colin Naslund, Debra Nothstein, Stacy Prenger, Bev Price, John Price, Rita Rambo, Gloria Reinheimer, Iris Scott, Joan Shaw, Jennette Stark, Brenda Slobodnick, Mercedes Smith, Sherry Springall, Anne Stang, Beryl Tankard, Donna Webster, Sari Weintraub, N. Ziemke, as well as many teachers in Sooke District (B.C.).

We also extend our appreciation to those teachers in Red Deer and in Ohio who attended our talks and gave suggestions. These include: Judy Bashforth, P. Buehler, Penelope Coughlin, Jody Dille, Janel Foolland, Becky Friedman, Joe Hayborgor, Julie Kurfis, Carol McKinley, Linda Miller, Janet Mueller, Kathy Neuman, Marcia Niehm, Sarah Pier, Beth Richer, Traci Schnipke, Linda Smith, Elaine Sommers, Jill Stubbs, Darlene Tressler, Elizabeth Waggoner and Bev Wolke.

Our philosophy has always been to include the ideas, strategies and resources we found ... and, if they got by Jennifer, they got in. A lot did! We are pleased!

Foreword: The Enticement of Information Books

Just give me the facts !

Kids who have become obsessed with facts or information and refuse to read about anything else are the focus of this book. Some Info-Kids are perfectly adequate readers, while others are not good at reading at all. Info-Kids who are reluctant to read may be astute readers who choose not to read and do not see the value of reading, or they can be struggling readers who have actual trouble reading text.

Students who are fascinated with nonfiction cannot be defined as a single group because they are too individualistic, too unique and too wide-ranging in their interests. Model builders, skateboarders, artists and card-collectors are all included, but there are many others. One of the characteristics that they share in common is a belief that fiction is not relevant in their lives. They will listen to stories read aloud in the classroom and share their own life stories, but as for sitting down and reading through a novel—forget it. It's not their kind of book.

Often, as teachers, we are prone to leave these students alone, almost help-lessly trying to entice them to read further afield. Frustration at the lack of change in their reading habits often results in a mutual negative non-learning truce. Although students may appear busy and are quiet, learning is often not accomplished.

In classrooms, Info-Kids have a tendency to get bored and restless. This does not occur as much in high-activity classes such as science or physical education, but language arts teachers are certainly aware of the danger in a "sit and read" situation.

At many conference presentations, especially after the publication of our book *Reluctant Readers,* teachers have asked us, "But my struggling readers only want the facts. How do I get past that?" The answer is quite simple—YOU WON'T!

Our goal is to have each student become aware and interested in the general topics of study. Our challenge is to tap into the children's interests and come up with strategies to keep them actively involved with the language arts curriculum and with others in the classroom. The best way may be to create a parallel curriculum. In this book we will explore ways to be successful in doing this.

Let's be realistic for a moment. What is the danger of students being absorbed in one topic? Nothing really! They may appear to be limited in their academic interests, but often they surprise us by how much they have absorbed. Actually, they have quietly been thinking, analyzing and categorizing. We must remember that today is only one moment in time in their school career. They could well change to a different interest next week, or their interests may turn into life-long, sustaining careers. Where do Info-Kids end up? That youngster who is the school's dinosaur expert may later be recognized as a leading paleontologist.

Info-Kids often become our computer programmers, mechanics, zoologists, plumbers, architects and potters of the future.

A perennial challenge is to find relevant information or nonfiction resources that will meet students' interests and reading ability. As has been shown, if students are interested in the topic, they will be able to read about it more proficiently than if they are not.

A great blessing for Info-Kids is the rapidly developing Internet—but don't be fooled into thinking it is the end-all and be-all. Students still need our assistance with search and location skills to be able to find material which is relevant. We can't allow them to get totally overwhelmed by the number of "hits" that often appear or to get "lost" in cyberspace. They also need help developing critical reading skills in order to be able to judge if the information is current and correct.

Using This Book

Our objective in writing this book is to share our belief that those students who are fascinated with facts—Info-Kids—are often actively engaged in learning on a variety of levels. It is their interest in a specific topic that motivates them to want to learn, and in many cases to realize that they need to read better. We as teachers should learn to go with the flow, recognizing and respecting the interest choices of the students, and creatively incorporating these in classroom activities based on engaging resources.

The Challenge of Info-Kids

In the first section of our book we begin by examining how to get Info-Kids jump-started with resources, by using perennial favorites. We then examine the various characteristics that Info-Kids may possess and the range in their approaches to learning. Next, we consider the importance of interest for all Info-Kids, but particularly for those who are reluctant readers.

Following that, we look at the types of information resources that are available and how to tell what constitutes a good information book. We have used the term *information book* most of the time, which we feel is less limiting than the traditional term *nonfiction*. Nonfiction signifies "not fiction," but does not entirely account for one of the major trends over the past decade, which has been the increased use of narrative accounts within nonfiction. Either term is acceptable though, and we do use both interchangeably.

Finally, we propose that teachers seriously consider initiating a parallel curriculum for Info-Kids. You may never get them to do the set curriculum, so why not be courageous and design one that will meet their needs?

The Reality of Info-Kids

In the second section of our book, eight chapters focus on eight main characteristics of Info-Kids and on how to use all eight to your instructional advantage.

We wanted to make this book relevant for teachers who are facing Info-Kids every day. Thus, we include a short list of typical characteristics of these Info-Kids, as well as a more detailed description. While we also present a list of

"Resources for Success," identifying those that are most likely to appeal to this type of Info-Kid is difficult to do. We recognize that Info-Kids are unpredictable in their choice of resources or topics. Our motto—if it works ... use it! Simply go with the flow.

Each Info-Kid is unique, both in interest and temperament. To honor this, we wanted to include descriptions of real kids. We asked teachers to tell us about students who could be described as being obsessed with facts and information. What are they like? What topics consume their interest? In what ways do they work well together? What resources are useful? What strategies work well to improve their reading and writing? In each of the eight chapters we feature two "Meet the Info-Kids" sketches of today's Info-Kids, as told to us by their teachers.

Each of the eight chapters also includes various types of strategies. Some strategies relate specifically to the interests of the type of Info-Kid being considered. It must be stated here that these are not recipes—activities of such a general nature that neither the student nor the teacher actually has to interact with a information book—but are rather integral links to and from a book or books. Remember that none of these are carved in stone and should be adapted to the circumstances. Other strategies relate to particular information resources that can help engage the interests that have been identified. Again, these are only starting points for finding and introducing excellent information resources to support learning.

Reading-thinking strategies are offered to focus on improving various types of thinking skills that affect reading ability. To be a good reader, we need to be able to associate, predict, infer, synthesize, analyze and monitor information. Info-Kids who are reluctant to read often have trouble using all of these thinking skills interactively, and can benefit from strategies like those offered in this book. Research-project strategies are also provided to assist Info-Kids in aspects of the process of seeking, organizing, editing and presenting information.

A further addition is a "Teacher Realities" section, designed to make us think about the differing levels underlying our teaching procedures. Teachers do need to increase their awareness and knowledge of characteristics of Info-Kids, their interests, information resources and suitable strategies for increasing literacy.

The Satisfaction of Working with Info-Kids

In the third and final section of our book, we consider diagnostic evaluation through the use of observation and checklists to indicate readers' interests and behaviors, how kids are thinking as they read, and whether we are doing a good job in teaching reading. We conclude the section by sharing some secrets of success that we have gleaned from our own experiences and those of our classroom teacher colleagues.

Marginalia and Sidebars

We couldn't help ourselves—we just had to tempt you with a few info-teasers (?) —intriguing questions related to interests explored in the core chapters. Sorry, none of them came from the *Guinness Book of Records!* As well, quotations from teachers, educators and authors, summaries of important points, and enticing information book lists are strategically placed in the margins and in sidebars.

Bibliographies

During the discussion of specific references throughout the book, publisher information has purposefully not been given. Consequently, a list of recommended titles is found at the back of the book. In the interest of relevance and currency, we have made an effort to include only those titles published since 1999, with the exception of some wonderful older favorites and a few classics. The list is not meant to be exhaustive, but rather a selective resource of those titles we have found to be valuable. Not all topics are covered. A limited number of narrative titles with a factual bent are also included. We consider this bibliography as a starting point—don't be limited by it. We have also included a concise professional bibiography for your consideration.

Part A: The Challenge of Info-Kids

Jump-Start

If you buy only one book for your classroom this year, choose the "Guinness Book of Records"!

Info-Kids are not renowned for their patience or their sit-still ability. They want to be turned loose to find out what they want to know about—now! So it is with this book—we wanted to focus immediately on the facts. Thus, we have selected four resources that are remarkable in luring Info-Kids, particularly those who are reluctant readers, because they have immense appeal.

Guinness Book of Records

The Appeal of the *Guinness Book of Records*

- Is here and now
- Is the best source for quirky, record-setting feats
- Publishes the most current achievements in the world
- Reflects current culture
- Establishes achievement levels
- Is reliable and accurate
- Is updated yearly
- Features "in-your-face" photos of people
- Uses short snippets of text
- Has a crisp writing style

This just might be the perfect gift for Dad and other guys! We have a long-time habit of giving friends who are dads this book for their birthday or celebrations such as Christmas. We know full well that it is usually immediately absconded by their sons and taken away to be devoured, only to reappear every few minutes along with gleeful excitement and comments about the person with the longest fingernails, the fastest tennis serve or the most wealth.

The rest of the visit is usually peppered with intense questions such as: "What is the highest waterfall in the world?"; "What is the biggest dinosaur?"; or "What is the most popular car?" The delicious smugness the child experiences over adults, through the power of knowing the answer ahead of time, is wondrous to witness. Knowing the facts gives control and delight.

Students have been attracted to this comprehensive compendium since its initial publication in 1955. To keep pace with today's visual generation, Guinness has gone FLASH! The current edition features multi-colored sections with dramatic photos and perspectives. The book's success is also attributable to its format of "communities of interest"; including achievement, danger, discovery, history, money, people, science, sport and urban. A remarkably detailed index is the crucial key to finding the records. It is absolutely crucial that every fall a new edition be purchased—$35 is not an excuse for students living in the twenty-first century to get facts from a 1985 edition!

The *Guinness Book of Records* is recognized as an adult book and, because of this, it is taken seriously and has much clout and believability. Remarkably, it has sold over 200 million copies in 23 languages.

A different dimension of this resource can be realized if its Web site is checked out (www.guinnessworldrecords.com).

Uncle John's All-Purpose Bathroom Reader

At several talks on challenging reluctant readers to read, we were approached by male teachers who said that if we wanted to get boys to become engaged in reading, we should get a copy of the *Bathroom Reader*—a regular feature in a particular room in their homes. Need we tell you what we gave for birthdays this year? It was an instant success!

The thirteenth edition of this book, published by the Bathroom Readers' Institute, is 495 pages packed with a hilarious assortment of short narratives, jokes, proverbs and quizzes. Part of the appeal is that so many facts are embedded in the stories, related to such topics as the episodes of several dumb crooks and how they were caught, classic hoaxes, movie bombs, time-cutting strategies to cut costs, ironic deaths, and how little things can mean a lot. Most appealing is that each section is a manageable one to three pages in length.

Consult the Web site (www.unclejohn.com) and, after literally opening the door the to the Bathroom Readers' Institute, you can enter the Throne Room, where, "flushed with excitement," you can read sample selections from the 14 books in the series.

> **We are a country of nonfiction readers.**
>
> *Betty Carter and Richard Abrahamson, educators*

The Way Things Work

David Macaulay's book *The Way Things Work* has achieved worldwide popularity and admiration, with over three million copies being sold in 19 languages. The detailed illustrations explaining the mechanics of movement, harnessing the elements, working with waves, as well as electricity and automation, will captivate even the Info-Kids who are most reluctant to read. It remains one of Houghton Mifflin's best sellers and is now available in a kit format with a CD-ROM, booklet, instruction cards and a toolbox.

Eyewitness and Beyond

In the last decade there has been a dramatic upheaval in the world of information/nonfiction books. This revolution can be credited to the *Eyewitness Guides* published by Dorling Kindersley. With the introduction of the first *Eyewitness Guide* in 1988, the world of information books has not been the same. Gone are dull formats with extensive text, black-and-white fuzzy photographs and overly simplistic, generalized illustrations. In are glossy, highly-visual pages on whiter-than-white paper, with short, succinct snippets of text and a multitude of highly-detailed, colored photographs.

There are now over 103 *Eyewitness Guides* in print, which have sold over 50 million copies in 88 countries and in 36 languages. The influence of new publishing partners, particularly Microsoft and Penguin Books, has kept the

Once the student realized that print held meaning, all fell into place.

April, teacher

momentum alive and resulted in older titles being revised. These "new" editions of this popular reference series, some with new titles, have been formatted with greater care to present content in an even more appealing and logical sequence. Always trying to intrigue the reader, Dorling Kindersley has also published a series of *3D Books,* tempting the student to use a one-sided mirror positioned in the centre of a narrow book to see small parts of life as we've never seen it before.

Another dramatic and successful series that Dorling Kindersley has created is the *DK Readers.* Based on the fact that many readers, particularly most boys, like their narrative stories filled with lots of facts, these books offer great potential for motivating Info-Kids to read. Some titles based on Lego characters are offered below.

Favorite DK Titles

Eyewitness Guides

- *Rocks and Minerals* by Chris Pellant
- *Spy* by Richard Platt
- *World War II* by Simon Adams
- *Arms and Armor* by Michele Byam

3-D Books

- *3-D Human Body* by Richard Walker
- *Microlife* by Theresa Greenaway
- *Space*
- *3-D Reptile* by A. Burton

DK Readers (based on Lego characters)

Level #1—Beginning to Read

- *Trouble at the Bridge* by Marie Birkinshaw
- *Secret at Dolphin Bay* by Marie Birkinshaw

Level #2—Beginning to Read Alone

- *Castle under Attack* by Nicola Baxter
- *Rocket Rescue* by Nicola Baxter

Level #3—Reading Alone

- *Mission to the Arctic* by Nicola Baxter

Level #4—Proficient Reader

- *Race for Survival* by Marie Birkinshaw

Finally, do not think about not having sufficient resources. Nobody has enough. Just introduce one of the titles mentioned in this chapter, put it in the middle of the table or on the floor, and sit back to enjoy what happens! You have started the irreversible process of releasing the energy and interest of the Info-Kids in your classroom.

CHAPTER 2

Who Are the Info-Kids?

We all know them—they drive us nuts while enhancing our lives!

Info-Kids are inherently active and physically proficient. These are the students who like arts and crafts, sports, constructing, model building and collecting—anything that requires "doing" or "making." Able to use their hands extremely well, they are good at manipulating materials and space. In the classroom we find them doodling, building inside their desks with Lego or straws, balancing on one leg of their chair, or displaying 14 different kinds of erasers or mini-cars lined up across the top of their desk.

Info-Kids are information seekers. Usually they either focus on a varied and ever-changing range of random facts, or permanently concentrate on one all-consuming topic. They are the analyzers of the world, always taking things apart, picking out the bits and honing in on the detail.

Info-Kids prefer to live in the "real world" around them and often do not see the value of literacy. Fiction's imaginary world does not appeal and the closest they will get to fiction is by choosing such reading materials as biographies, documentaries, natural history chronicles, and sometimes the more technically-focused and reality-based versions of science fiction. Although many do not like to read or write, they can be great talkers about themselves and their interests.

Most Info-Kids are boys, yet a small proportion turn out to be girls. This is because in our society boys are inculcated to, and expect to be rewarded by, looking outside themselves. Girls, on the other hand, are expected to be inward, feeling-focused and people-oriented. Most comply. Some girls, however, march to a different drummer, preferring an outward, world-oriented direction to their thoughts and interests. Regardless of gender, the focus of Info-Kids is on real objects in our world rather than on fictional characters in an imaginary one.

Info-Kids have their own agenda, which is often different from the classroom's. Their inner rhythms, time schedules and interests do not easily fit with the classroom's set curriculum. We as teachers must accept these Info-Kids as they are, recognize the validity of their passions and take an interest in their topics, rather than expect them to be interested in ours. Who knows? We might learn more than we bargained for … and feel better about our teaching too!

There's no such thing as a kid who doesn't want to read; there is only a kid who hasn't met the right book.
Sari, teacher

Characteristics of Info-Kids

- Physically active
  - Prefer hands-on activities
  - Play sports

- Good at manipulating materials
  - Enjoy arts and crafts, construction, model building, collections, etc.

- Information seekers
  - Love random facts
  - Focus on one topic, then another

- Fact finders
  - Delight in taking things apart
  - Pick things out

- Literacy procrastinators
  - Do not like to write or read
  - Can be talkers

- Fiction avoiders
  - Prefer to live in the "real world"

- Mostly boys
  - Focus on objects in outside "real world"
  - Reflect our culture
  - Are physically active

- Occasionally girls
  - Choose non-traditional roles
  - March to a different drummer

- Have their own agenda
  - Establish a personal inner rhythm
  - Live by a unique time schedule
  - Display idiosyncratic interests
  - Prefer to be involved with world outside of classroom

Info-Kids Who Are Reluctant to Read

The information-oriented kids in our classrooms fall into very separate categories when it comes to reading ability. There are the Info-Kids who enjoy reading and have no trouble with it at all. Then there are two types of reluctant readers.

One type of reluctant reader can read quite proficiently, "thank you very much," but is just not inclined to bother. Having this aliterate attitude, reading and writing are not things that interest them, nor that they do willingly. There are so many more interesting things to do—things that are more important, more fun and more rewarding. Why take the trouble?

The second type of reluctant reader includes those that are truly struggling with reading. Not only are they not interested in reading, they simply can't do it well. Showing interest in other things besides literacy gives them a social "out" and salves their self-concept. Their diversity of interests frequently gives them an advantage with their peers that their reading does not. These students particularly benefit from the format of information books because they process the content by using visual and non-visual cues.

Info-Kids who are reluctant to read include both kinds, thus strategies and resources must be flexible enough to interest both types. All of the strategies included in this book can be made simpler or more complex to fit a particular student's needs. Our basic assumption, and one becoming more and more evi-

> More experience with non-narrative texts in the early grades may help mitigate the difficulties many students encounter with these texts later in schooling.
> *Linda Caswell and Nell Duke, educators and researchers*

dent to reading experts, is that the most effective way to teach a struggling reader is the same way we teach any developing reader—start from where they are and do whatever helps them improve their reading.

The Challenges of Info-Kids Who Are Reluctant to Read

As he started the book he struggled a bit, and I pointed out a few words he had seen/read before. Then it was like a light went on and because he really wanted to read the book, he started to realize that he already knew and recognized most of the words. This was when he started to get excited about reading. It is now a year later and I often see him reading for pleasure.
Diane, teacher

To become skillful readers, Info-Kids who are reluctant to read must overcome a number of beliefs and habits that hold them back. These readers believe they can't read partly because reading to them is just related to reading stories and not the kind of reading they do—browsing short snippets and seeking facts and information.

They also believe writing is too difficult, too complex and too complicated. Although they often have much to say, particularly about topics that they have invested time and effort in, they balk at putting pen to paper. Feeling inadequate about handwriting, spelling, or composition and organization skills, these Info-Kids are overcome when attempting the intricacies of writing.

Often the way they deal with their believed inadequacies is through distracting their teacher with unproductive, unacceptable classroom behavior, either by acting out or hiding out. Both being overactive or passive is intended to allow them to ignore and avoid what goes on around them. Since, for children, behavior is communication, we have to see this "bad" behavior as a coping skill due most often to unease with literacy and lack of interest in classroom topics. In the case of such Info-Kids, disruptive or secretive behavior is a symptom, not a disease.

The set curriculum required in most classrooms doesn't help—instead it exacerbates the problem. Such a curriculum can be dull and unexciting for children who are not reluctant readers, let alone for those who are. If done in a rote, textbook sort of way, science, social studies and literature can be made boring with a vengeance. Is it any wonder we end up labeling many reluctant readers with an attention deficit disorder? We too would have a short attention span if confronted with the uninteresting content and methods encountered in some classrooms.

Info-Kids have minds filled with facts, indeed with bits and pieces of knowledge they have gleaned through analyzing all they encounter. Picking out facts and taking content apart are easy kinds of thinking for them and tend to be the only ones they practise. As their teachers, we need to help them become fluent thinkers beyond the literal level. Our job is to help them learn to use with ease the associating, predicting, inferring, synthesizing and monitoring forms of thinking. Plus, we need to help them learn to relate the "facts" they covet and know to the curriculum they are faced with in our classrooms.

In researching motivating children to read, I came across the social value that reading has. If avid readers socialize with reluctant readers, those reluctant readers become avid readers.
Renata, teacher

Many Info-Kids dread the hugeness of a big project, whether it ends in a presentation or as a written report. The whole drawn-out process of finding, categorizing, drawing together, organizing, summarizing, and especially putting it all down on paper overwhelms them. They give up and dwell instead in the realm of small bits and pieces. Our task is to help them see how the whole project can be divided into the small bits and chunks they can cope with, while assisting them to work their way through the process one piece at a time.

In actual fact, Info-Kids' thinking abilities are no different than the rest of the class. The only real difference is that they do not like to read or they believe they cannot read. However, they are different in that they prefer to focus on the real world, frequently on one specific topic. It is our job as teachers to bring those outside interests inside the classroom and allow them to become a valued part of the curriculum.

Obstacles Reluctant Readers May Have to Overcome

- Their beliefs
  - I can't read
  - Reading is just about reading stories
  - Writing is too difficult
  - We don't do anything fun in school

- Set curriculum
  - Curriculum that is decided by somebody else
  - Lessons that are dull and boring
  - Content that is not interesting

- Short attention span
  - Disinterest
  - Lack of challenge
  - Lack of commitment
  - Isolation

- Acting-out/hiding-out behaviors
  - Demonstrations of disinterest
  - Coping mechanism(s)
  - Symptoms that are not the problem

- Fact-filled minds
  - "Literal" thinking
  - Difficulty in thinking in other ways
  - Inability to relate "facts" to classroom needs

- Dread of big projects
  - Writing
  - Being overwhelmed by the size
  - The organization of such an undertaking
  - The skills involved in drawing everything together

CHAPTER 3

Interest Is Paramount

Here today, gone tomorrow!

It has often been said that interest defines the person. Interest motivates curiosity, mastery and drive, and empowers the will to succeed. As teachers we know that the secret for success in school does not depend on intellectual ability alone, but rather on the forces motivating students. We give our hearty thanks to Harry Potter! May he long interest reluctant readers and their peers.

In working with Info-Kids, particularly those who are reluctant to read, it is our experience that:

- There are an incredible variety of interests, with no end to the kinds of things kids can get interested in
- Interest reflects students' background and experience
- Connecting to interest is more powerful than anything else we can do as teachers
- Interest can be tailored to each student—whatever facet they are taken with can be used to instruct
- Interest drives learning for reluctant readers more than for other kinds of kids
- Interest allows students to ignore that they are learning to read and write
- Interest allows teachers to hide literacy skills so kids don't balk
- Interest gives students control and choice over materials
- Interest reflects the influence of parents, family, friends and particularly peers

Reluctant readers come to school with a predetermined set of interests, frequently reflecting the interests of Dad, Mom, big brother or sister, and maybe aunts and uncles. Interests are formed in part by family holidays, excursions, sporting and cultural events, as well as by family television viewing habits. Increasingly important is the ready access to the use of the family computer and free time to surf the net.

As teachers we must recognize the reality that interest is the way into the set curriculum. Unless we go with the flow of their interests, we will only be struggling against the outgoing tide! Allowing ourselves to be flexible and willing to adapt class projects and assignments to incorporate the interests of Info-Kids who are reluctant to read should result in successful involvement by all. If defined generally enough, many students of varying abilities can focus on aspects of the same topic at different levels of commitment.

Curiosity is one of the permanent and certain characteristics of a vigorous intellect. Every advance into knowledge opens new prospects and produces new excitement to further progress.
Samuel Johnson, English author and critic

Determining Interests

Classic Topics of Interest
- Dinosaurs
- Space
- Hockey
- Horses
- War
- Middle Ages

What are Info-Kids who are reluctant to read interested in? A tough question. We should not be deceived by an obvious response when we ask, "What are you interested in?" or "What do you like to read about?" If we get the obvious everybody-likes-hockey answer, we must realize that students may cover up real interests to save face and avoid the risk of you, and everyone else listening, knowing them that deeply. The greatest challenge we have as teachers is to get below the obvious and find out their real interests.

Reluctant readers may be hiding what they are truly interested in. If they have been put down in the class or at home, they may feel the topic is not valuable or feel ashamed of wanting to know about it. It is our task to find out what they really want to know and then value it. Yet it takes astute digging to find out. To do so, we must adopt strategies that will help "mine" those interests. How do we do this? There are three good ways:

- *Active listening*—We must improve and practise our active listening both in the classroom and on the playground. Hints are dropped in snippets throughout conversations and interactions. Most often it is during quiet non-directed activities that we can detect clues from unsolicited comments.
- *Active viewing*—We must watch what types of resources Info-Kids select and what they are surfing for on the Web. One strategy is to give individual students a pile of new books, or those you think might interest them, and watch how they browse through them. Which do they open? Which do they discard immediately? Always include some unexpected titles because you just never know.
- *Constant attention*—We must become more aware of current fads that influence student interests. For example, what is the latest on Harry, Pokeman, wrestling or YTV? Being classed as the purveyors of "good" literature and "acceptable" interests simply because we as teachers are the authorities, should not stop us from moving beyond that role. Let's realize that the "junk" is just a passing fad and will eventually be put aside for better things.

When students are allowed to read something that interests them, substantial reading growth often can be seen.
Sandra McCormick,
reading clinician and educator

Developing Interests

Interests change—what Info-Kids are interested in today may not be the topic of attention tomorrow. Be ready to allow changes in topic and to discard one if it does not appear to be working. We cannot allow ourselves to invest too much emotionally or intellectually in any one scenario. It is better to be flexible, and to watch and enjoy the moment. A current interest may fade away totally, or more excitingly, become a bridge to a more lasting interest.

Interests are not always about animals or space or cars. In other words, interests may not always be about content. Instead they could be related to peer pressure, as in *Harry Potter;* or to language, such as scientific jargon or jokes; or to a natural aptitude, such as model making, sports or playing a musical instrument. There is no end to where interests come from and what they will be about.

When a child's concentration while reading is based on enjoyment and interest this intense, the result is a loss of self-consciousness, which can be extremely liberating, both cognitively and emotionally.

Rosalie Fink,
reading researcher

Interests are not only about fads, but an awareness of current fads, and interest in them, is important because Info-Kids are interested in what is happening in the world around them. Earthquakes, dust blowing from the China Desert circling the entire globe, the Olympics, the Stanley Cup Championship or the latest scientific advance all have potential.

To tap into interests, whatever they happen to be, and to use them to advance reluctant readers' literacy abilities, means we must learn to be sneaky in trying to fit those interests into the classroom curriculum, to broaden Info-Kids' spectrum of interests and to try occasionally connecting to the world of fiction. Where there is a will there is a way. We as teachers must keep in mind that the way is through interest.

CHAPTER 4

Engaging Information Resources

Not all resources are equal!

We are in the golden age of information books for young readers as evidenced by the dramatic improvement in appealing and worthwhile books on a vast range of topics. Students, technically, have more information books available to them today than ever before. This may not be the case in all schools as it depends on the selection ability of the teacher-librarian.

Are information books valued in the classroom? Our hidden curriculum becomes readily observable to Info-Kids, and in many situations it is evident that narrative has the upper hand when it comes to acceptability. We need to ask: Are students allowed to read information books during reading time? Why should only fiction titles be given the green light? Once students see that information/nonfiction books are acceptable, they will start to feel better about reading them. Our objective, after all, is to get students reading and actively involved in the reading process.

One of the best ways to encourage Info-Kids to read information books is to read segments aloud on a regular basis! Don't feel compelled to read the entire book, when chapters or short sections will serve the purpose just as well.

In an information age, where the appeal of information in the media cannot be denied, it is surprising to note the number of poor quality books that are readily available and being bought by unsuspecting/indiscriminating teachers and parents.

Out-of-date and inaccurate information in any resource is *dangerous to the mental health of youngsters*! There can be no excuse for having books which state that one day we may land on the moon, or which contain accounts of non-existing dinosaurs such as the brontosaurus or out-of-date maps, particularly of Africa and Russia.

The perennial excuse of professionals for keeping these resources, including any encyclopedias over five years old, in the school library is that parts of them are useful. The question then becomes: Who is going to be there to tell the student which information is correct and which is erroneous? This assumes that the teacher is available and will know! Students have the right to be taught the truth—not incorrect information! We cannot afford to be teaching with out-of-date materials (and don't even think of sending them to kids in Africa!).

The challenge is in how to teach students to figure the facts out for themselves by cross-checking the dates of materials, checking the references of authors and being critical about the content itself. It is crucial that a constant

Information Resources

- Reference books (encyclopedias, almanacs, dictionaries)
- Single topic information books
- Picture books for older readers
- Biographies, autobiographies, journals, diaries
- CD-ROMs
- CD encyclopedias
- Artifacts
- Newspapers
- Magazines
- Instruction manuals
- Guides
- Books on tape
- Internet
- Brochures, pamphlets (travel, business, hotels, government, parks, etc.)

What Attracts Info-Kids to Information Books?

- Bright colors
- Eye-catching illustrations on the cover
- Appealing illustrations
- Intriguing realistic illustrations
- Interesting photographs
- Lots of details in photographs
- Awesome size of illustrations or photographs
- Small chunks of text
- Not too much text on a page
- The choice of how to read the page
- Activities allowing for interaction with the book's content
- Links to the Internet

Sure Turn-Offs

- An overdose of text on a page
- Fuzzy illustrations
- Unillustrated cover (book jacket may be missing)
- A book that is too thick
- Very little space to breathe (too much on each page)

weeding program is in place, in order to keep the school library resource centre collection relevant. This is particularly crucial in those shocking situations where schools do not have a professional teacher-librarian. The level of professionalism and quality of instruction is negatively affected when available resources are inaccurate and out-of-date. We must assume responsibility for the resources we use.

What Do Teachers Need to Know about Information Books?

There are an overwhelming number of information/ nonfiction books available today. Not all of them are high quality. Thus, it is important that we know how to select the best from them, as all are definitely not equal. Content is of primary concern, as is style of writing, visual appeal and ease of use. When assessing the value of a book for your classroom, consider whether it:

- Is accurate (if not—get rid of it!)
- Is up to date (If not—discard it!)
- Includes an index (if not—don't buy it!)
- Presents information clearly and directly (if not—don't buy it!)
- Includes illustrations/photos which enhance and extend the text
- Features captions which clearly explain the illustrations, diagrams and photographs
- States the qualifications of the author
- Clarifies its purpose
- Is written appropriately for the intended audience
- Has a clear structure for presenting information
- Contains a glossary, appendix and a table of contents
- Includes a bibliography for future research
- Includes headings for ease of locating information
- Gives Internet links
- Has drawings that actually look like people!

Information/Nonfiction Awards

We all need to have resources available to us to assist us in recognizing fine quality information books. At long last, awards have been created to recognize excellence in the creation of information books for young readers.

In Canada, *The Information Book Award* has been given annually since 1985 by the Children's Literature Roundtables of Canada. This award is administered by the Vancouver Roundtable and is voted on by the many Children's Literature Roundtables across Canada. The announcement of the winner is made in early November, in time for Canadian Children's Book Week.

In the United States, the *Orbis Pictus Award* is given for outstanding nonfiction for children by the National Council of Teachers of English. The literary criteria is based on accuracy, organization, design and style. Furthermore, according to its Web site (www.ncte.org), each book "... should be useful in classroom teaching (grades K-8), and should encourage thinking and more reading, model exemplary expository writing and research skills, share interesting and timely subject matter, and appeal to a wide range of ages." In Australia, the Children's Book Council gives the *Eve Pownall Award for Information Books*, recognizing the finest in nonfiction for young people.

Information Book Award Winners (Canada)

(2001)   *The Kid's Book of Canada's Railway and How the CPR Was Built* by Deborah Hodge
(2000)   *Wow Canada! Exploring This Land from Coast to Coast to Coast* by Vivien Bowers
(1999)   *The Last Safe House: A Story of the Underground Railroad* by Barbara Greenwood
(1998)   *The Buried City of Pompeii* by Shelley Tanaka
(1997)   *On Board the Titanic* by Shelley Tanaka
(1996)   *In Flanders Fields* by Linda Granfield

Orbis Pictus Award Winners (United States)

(2001)   *Hurry Freedom: African Americans in Gold Rush California* by Jerry Stanley
(2000)   *Through My Eyes* by Ruby Bridges and Margo Lundell
(1999)   *Shipwreck at the Bottom of the World: The Extraordinary True Story of Schackleton and the Endurance* by Jennifer Armstrong
(1998)   *An Extraordinary Life: The Story of a Monarch Butterfly* by Laurence Pringle
(1997)   *Leonardo da Vinci* by Diane Stanley
(1996)   *The Great Fire* by Jim Murphy

Eve Pownall Award for Information Books (Australia)

(2001)   *Olympia: Warrior Athletes of Ancient Greece* by Dyan Blacklock
(2000)   *Fishing for Islands: Traditional Boats and Seafarers of the Pacific* by John Nicholson
(1999)   *Going for Kalta: Hunting for Sleepy Lizards at Yalata* by Yvonne Edwards and Brenda Day
(1998)   *A Home among Gum Trees: The Story of Australian Houses* by John Nicholson
(1997)   *Killer Plants and How to Grow Them* by Gordon Cheers and Julie Silk
(1996)   *The First Fleet: A New Beginning in an Old Land* by John Nicholson

How Do Teachers Evaluate the Internet?

In weighing the pros and cons of placing struggling students within electronic environments, teachers may feel inclined to shelter such readers by exposing them only to print. Such a strategy would remove the navigational perils of hypertext and the confusing array of supportive resources, but it would also deny them the advantages of that support.

Michael McKenna et al.,
educators and researchers

In the history of educational resources, television was going to be the panacea for every academic program, then it was video and, most recently, it is the computer. This is just not true as there is still a major lack of hardware. Although CD encyclopedias appear exciting, they can only be used by one student at a time unless the school has a CD-ROM server with multi-user access. This is in sharp contrast to many students looking at different volumes of a book set.

Is the Internet the answer? Too many technology-impressed and money-conscious administrators will tell you it is—yet, can they find information when challenged? The Web does contain an awesome amount of information, much of which is current and up to date, but a lot is not. As we surf the Web we must develop an ever-present skeptical attitude, questioning if content is correct. Why? Too often we do not know the qualifications of those who have posted the information, and we do not know if the content is accurate or up to date. Beware of the bells and whistles! Many sites are wonderfully visual and appealing, but what is really there? Students must be trained to be critical of sites they visit and to expand their visual literacy skills.

We must also realize that students need to practise their research/locational skills on books first before they get lost in cyberspace. This is why knowledge of how to use an index is crucial for the successful hunt for facts. Review with students how to use a book to get information, outlining the appropriate steps. First, students must be clear as to what they want to find out. Can they narrow their topic down or do they need to broaden it? What are appropriate descriptive terms which might help? Second, students need to be taught how to use the format features of different references that can assist in the search. Third, students should be asked to consult several sources for information on the topic and compare the results of each. In doing this, students can be encouraged to comment on which resource was most valuable and why.

It is becoming increasingly obvious that more and more Info-Kids are not taking in or absorbing the information they find on the Internet. It is all too easy—they look at the screen, then simply press the key to print, and out it comes. Sometimes they even turn this material in as their report. We need to keep a watchful eye on this practice, or else arrange for small group sessions to work through what one does with information after one finds it.

What Info-Kids Need to Watch Out for on the Internet

- Becoming lost in cyberspace (Where am I? Where is it?)
- Outdated information
- Incorrect information
- Lifted or stolen information
- Difficulty in locating an appropriate site (search skills)
- Changing and inconsistent search engines, each with different access patterns
- The ability to return to information and/or the site later
- Lack of accurate information

When one is trying to establish criteria for a good Web site, it is crucial to consult an excellent resource such as the Schrock Guide site (www.school.discovery.com/schrockguide/eval.html). This contains a critical evaluation survey for elementary kids to fill out and a good section on how to set up a content-rich Web page, including a valuable section on how to get your site linked to others for a greater reach.

The Cyberbee site listed by Schrock is designed for teachers rather than kids, and it actually leads to an overall point evaluation. Two resources are highlighted, featuring their criteria for sites. The University of Maryland looks at: scope, authority, bias, accuracy, timeliness, permanence, value-added features and presentation. The University of Albany looks at: purpose, source, content, style and functionality. Encourage your Info-Kids to establish their own criteria.

What Attracts Info-Kids to the Internet?	**What Do Teachers Need to Know about the Internet?**
• It is right here and now • Students are in control • Colors and sounds have all sorts of bells and whistles • It is fun, lively and motivating • It allows for active participation • It is easy to follow (click and flow) • Students can select the sequence and pick and choose where they go • Students can ignore what they don't want • It is highly visual and aural • Sites are often up to date for current topics • There are an incredible number of sites to visit • It offers an interactive multimedia experience • Students can find information on just about everything	• Is a site up to date? • Who created a site? What is the expertise of the person entering the data? • Is a site accurate and correct? • Do we understand the basics and are we prepared to become co-adventurers? • Will we be able to be there to facilitate if there is only one computer in the classroom? • How much time is spent hunting for information? • How much time is required to teach every child to use it? • What do the kids actually do? Is the focus on content or on guessing? Are the activities merely games? • Is the readability level developmentally appropriate? Do the students have the reading skills to use the Internet? • Are effective information literacy skills in place?

A final word on resources. Use what is available but dump the junk! There is no longer ample money in school-based programs for resources, print or otherwise. Therefore, we must be wiser in our selections for purchase. The need for information books is greater than ever, particularly if students are given a greater degree of freedom to select and research topics that interest them. It is our responsibility, in conjunction with the teacher-librarian, to know what is available in the school and to assess it for accuracy or currency. The weeding process must be continuous as new information is found. As two thirds of the school library resource centre collection will be nonfiction/information books, it is important to have a vital collection. Similarly, it is essential that we assist students in learning how to navigate the Internet and develop skills for assessing the information they find there in order to competently use this resource.

Any time I start a new unit, I always go to the library to find books, magazines, maps, Internet sites, newspaper articles, etc. to coincide with that particular unit. Whenever I see my students going to the chalk tray to look at or read these items, I know I've touched their heart.

Rita, teacher

CHAPTER 5

A Parallel Curriculum

Get real!

No matter what you want them to do, Info-Kids who are not readers will not cover your curriculum and your curriculum will not cover them. What we want does not necessarily equal what they want. To include them, we need to change the curriculum so it better fits their needs. One thing that interferes with a match between the set curriculum and Info-Kids who are reluctant to read is that, until at least grade four, we tend to focus on narrative, and not on information. Since these students don't like narrative, they ignore it, and by doing so lose their first chance at learning reading skills.

What is it that you want to know?
Marion Crook, writer

Fortunately, for any child, the process of learning is more important that any particular curriculum content. No one child in a classroom retains the same content out of what is taught anyway. Day in and day out, each and every student focuses on what catches his or her attention and simply ignores the rest. It is not the content that students take away from the curriculum we teach, but rather it is the process of thinking and the processes of learning to read and write that are most important. And those processes, particularly with Info-Kids who are reluctant readers, are what we must focus on. Any content (curriculum) of interest can allow us to teach the process of reading. However, the content must be of interest to the Info-Kid or there will be no desire to learn.

Addressing the Myths of the Curriculum

Frequently certain beliefs are maintained, rightly or wrongly, regarding the significance of the set curriculum. These include the following:

- The set curriculum is sacred and all of it must be done
- Every child gets from the set curriculum the same information and skills
- Curriculum that is teacher-directed is more effective
- The teacher's role is to get through the set curriculum
- The creators of the set curriculum are better able to construct the right curriculum than the classroom teacher
- The set curriculum is current

As teachers, we have been taught to believe we must always get through all the curriculum for each subject. Plus, we are faced with more being added constantly to what we must teach. This leads to an acceleration in pace and the time pressure becomes overwhelming. Info-Kids tend to not keep up with the pace because they are not interested in the content, and often their own sense of time does not fit with our need to hurry. With Info-Kids who are reluctant readers, our only hope is to step back and ignore the "needs" of the curriculum and pay attention to the "needs" of the reluctant reader.

It is more important to teach literacy skills than subject content. Literacy skills include learning to:

- Focus on meaning, not only at the literal level, but also at the inferential and critical levels
- Self-correct through awareness at the metacognitive level
- Use meaning, language structure and graphophonics to figure out words

Indeed, if teachers want to help Info-Kids read and write better, they can let them learn literacy skills through their interests. More sneakily, they can search out what is of interest and connect this to the curriculum. In this way, a parallel curriculum is created.

What is a parallel curriculum? Basically, the teacher's task is to focus on the literacy and research skills which impact the students in the classroom. It is process over content. There can be great variability in the topic and scope of projects, but the basics of the research process or reading skills are still being covered. More confident teachers will allow several students to undertake independent studies. Broad topics such as the environment, endangered species or global warming can offer great potential for smaller, more focused explorations.

Remembering that kids only learn about what they are interested in, our task is to seek out relevant content which intrigues rather than mandates their attention. Otherwise, if their only interest at school is recess, then that is all they are going to learn. Interests and resources obviously go together, thus it is also important for teachers to provide a great variety of resources.

For Info-Kids who are reluctant to read and write, the task is to learn the literacy skills they are missing. When they are focused on content that interests them, learning to read and write happens without concentrating on the process and without effort. Learning to read and write is, in essence, subsumed within alluring content and ignored while it happens.

Thinking Skills Needed by Info-Kids

Students need to use all possible thinking modes interactively and simultaneously, rather than depend on only one kind of thinking as many Info-Kids who are reluctant readers do. For them, analyzing and breaking things down into parts is the easy and the automatic way of thinking. Yet, within the skill of analyzing, these Info-Kids can have trouble selecting out the most important details needed for true understanding. This leads to not being able to make the needed connections and pull together the important details to create summaries and generalizations. These are the kinds of students who take apart a clock but cannot sort through the pieces and put it back together again. For these students, the

Being an astronaut was very exciting because I was able to see things for myself that I had wondered about and studied as a child. Sometimes our childhood interests determine our work as adults. It is very important to really care about the work you choose to do.

Sally Ride, American astronaut/writer quoted in Flora Wyatt

skills of associating (making connections) and synthesizing (putting pieces together) are not easy.

Likewise, predicting (educated guessing) or inferring (filling in the gaps) are not easy either. Info-Kids who have difficulty with reading can find these two reading-thinking processes particularly difficult. Nonfiction, the type of material they prefer to read, requires analysis but very little inference, prediction, association or synthesis type thinking. The facts are stated clearly and concisely in this type of material.

With some Info-Kids who are reluctant to read, another thinking process, monitoring (self-checking), is almost non-existent. Some can see and correct their mistakes, but most can not. Being able to analyze and to recognize details can help them hone in on correcting, but it is not guaranteed. The use of this kind of thinking while reading or writing, along with the other reading-thinking processes, must be taught.

This lack of flexibility in thinking is why the research process itself can be a stumbling block for Info-Kids who are reluctant readers. Locating, analyzing, organizing, summarizing and presenting information requires putting many details together and so can seem overwhelming in its complexity.

Employing critical thinking skills is not something most Info-Kids do well either. Making judgments about the value, the validity and the intent of a piece of writing demands skills they do not use easily. Evaluation of Web sites, information books and author reliability all ask for complex critical thinking—thinking they are not generally adept at.

Skills Needed by Teachers of Info-Kids

For us as teachers, the point is to teach the literacy skills that Info-Kids who are reluctant to read need through making the curriculum relevant enough for them to pay attention. The best way to do this is by making a connection between Info-Kids' interests and the set curriculum.

This means we must be acutely perceptive of students' true interests and must become active listeners groping for keen understanding. We must provide the background knowledge for Info-Kids to make connections and be responsible for showing students how the knowledge they have and enjoy relates to classroom and curriculum content. By continually seeking resources related to student interests, we can provide the thought-provoking artifacts and multimedia materials that reinforce their learning and provide the parallel curriculum they require. As well, we need to continue asking intriguing higher-level questions, become aware of which literacy processes are difficult for our students, and begin to make more connections between nonfiction and fiction to broaden their interests and understanding.

The continuing challenge for teachers is to provide:

- Stimulating connections to the set curriculum
  - Seek "deep" interests
  - Mine and underline interests
  - Detect and accept changes of interest

Children interview, record, and write because they will need the information again—for themselves and for the many audiences who will find the data useful.

Donald Graves,
educator and researcher

If I let them take charge of their own learning, they accomplish so much more.

Joan, teacher

Interactive Reading-Thinking Processes

The many interactive reading-thinking processes that all readers require include:

- Analyzing strategies
  – Picking out the pieces
  – Identifying all the parts
  – Seeing all the bits

- Synthesizing strategies
  – Combining details into a new concept
  – Putting parts back into a coherent whole
  – Paraphrasing, summarizing and seeing the relationships between bits such as the sequences, causes and effects, comparisons or contrasts
  – Finding the main idea, main point, theme, moral

- Associating strategies
  – Making connections
  – Categorizing
  – Connecting words with meaning

- Predicting strategies
  – Making educated guesses
  – Hypothesizing
  – Telling what happens next

- Inferring strategies
  – Filling in the gaps left by the author
  – Picking out unstated information
  – Combining background knowledge with the text

- Monitoring strategies
  – Self-correcting
  – Developing meta-cognitive awareness
  – Seeing mistakes and fixing them

- Research process strategies
  – Locating information
  – Analyzing information
  – Organizing information
  – Summarizing information
  – Presenting
  – Employing critical thinking strategies
  – Evaluating Web sites
  – Evaluating information books
  – Evaluating author reliability

By giving students a significant amount of freedom to choose the topics, tasks and media for learning, teachers enable students to take ownership of their growth as a learner.

John Guthrie and Ann McCann, educators and researchers

- Links to background knowledge and interests
  - Provide access to resources
  - Seek varied resources
  - Bring in thought-provoking artifacts
- Provocative questions
  - Employ a diversity of question types
  - Focus on inferential and critical questions
  - Ask some questions with no "right" answer
  - Ask some questions with no answers at all
- An encouraging atmosphere
  - Offer flexibility and choice
  - Accept changes in direction
  - Normalize differences
- Connections to fiction and other genres
  - Link real-world situations to stories
  - Find informational interests within fiction
  - Find humorous interests within fiction

It takes belief and courage to implement a parallel curriculum. The challenge is to try something different and to believe that through allowing these Info-Kids to follow their own interests, and to incorporate thinking skills, they will improve their reading ability and learn equally as much—if not more!

Part B: The Reality of Info-Kids

CHAPTER 6

Info-Kids Who Are Outward-Focused

Let go! I know how ... !

Characteristics

- Look outward to the "real world"
- Model themselves on externally-focused adults
- Orientated to sports and games
- Seek competition

Resources for Success

- Newspapers
- Magazines
- Sports books
- Sports biographies
- How-to-do-things books
- Game rule books

Many Info-Kids are outward-focused. Frequently these are boys who are concerned with what is happening out in the world. Their interests are a reflection of a distinctive approach to the world which focuses on external happenings and objects. These students want to know what is going on out there and want to be involved in it, whatever it is. Often their interest shows up as an interest in sports as many of them have a good sense of balance, which they take glee in showing by teetering on one leg on the top of a wall or edge of a wharf.

We should not underestimate the importance of fathers and male teachers on these Info-Kids. Adult males exhibit many of the same characteristics as do these outward-focused male students. The difference may be only in that many adult males have been very successful in integrating their interests with their work and life, while interfacing with the literacy demands made by the world. More use should be made of these adults as mentors and models. Boys, in particular, need to see older males who enjoy reading and writing.

Even though most are boys, there is a small proportion of girls who exhibit these characteristics too. In our culture, an outward focus is expected of boys, while, on the other hand, girls are assumed to be inward-looking, feeling-focused and people-oriented. Some girls don't fit into this traditional cultural model, instead preferring to make or manipulate things and to focus on physical happenings or outside events. These girls need to be allowed to be the information gatherers they are and not be expected to be fiction-oriented just because they are girls.

Meet the Info-Kids

Michael—Zines Shoot and Score!

Michael loves hockey. He plays on a hockey team outside of school, and enjoys watching it on TV and going to games with his dad. Michael's interest is so keen that he reads the paper regularly to keep up to date on his favorite players and teams, and the stats. Every day he has a hockey magazine that he reads in class. Although he is not able to read all the words, he finds ways to get the information that he wants, such as using headlines and picture clues, and reading with his friends.

The power of his interest ... in hockey ... is a strong motivator, and the magazines provide an accessible way for him to pursue that interest, which in turn drives his skill building in a real and meaningful way.

Debra, teacher

Magazines provide a way for Michael to interact with other boys in the class and have become a springboard to motivate his writing. Often he does not write, but instead spends long periods of time copying stories in his journal or on his laptop, which he then rereads and shares. He has now begun to extend his research on the Internet and to edit his writing both with classmates and on his own.

Luc—Extreme Sports

Luc is into extreme sports. He has just come through a long period of only being willing to check out books about motocross racing. As the school library only had five books on the topic, he had read them all several times. He pestered the teacher-librarian until she was able to get him switched to snowboarding and other extreme sports. The teacher-librarian even purchased a whole new set of books on extreme sports. Luc came every day to see if more had arrived. During the winter he wore his snow pants inside school all day. Drove his teacher nuts!

Focus on Interests

Join the Team—and Succeed!

Sports receive major coverage in newspapers and on televisions. Sports stars are probably the best paid performers in the world, easily surpassing Hollywood movie stars. Many video games also reflect this sports obsession. When outward-focused Info-Kids are encouraged to engage in after-school activities, the majority choose sports—martial arts, gymnastics, swimming or team sports, to name a few. For greater success in the classroom, link strategies with the playing field.

Strategy—Go for Broke! What's the Record?

Hockey and baseball cards have been a source of popularity over the generations. Today they are still a source of delight, and enthusiasts of either game will probably have amassed an impressive collection. Let's challenge the students to go beyond just having a binder full of cards; let's get them comparing players, teams and years.

Start with superlatives—who's the best ... the most ... the largest? The worst? The lowest? Who has the most home runs ... the most hits ... the most shut-outs ... the most assists? Look at the records—which are the ones to meet? To beat? Looking ahead, not just behind, have the students extrapolate what they feel is possible in the future and what improvements have been made over the years. Can you find adult enthusiasts to come and share their views with the class? How to share this information? Graphs show it all!

Strategy—What! You Didn't See It?

Kids like to use sports lingo a lot. They have their favorite sports broadcasters, and many of them are able to do quite impressive imitations of them. Great! Put this talent to use! Encourage them to become a radio/TV commentator for a playoff sporting event.

Using the lingo of the sport, students can tape-record the broadcast for later sharing in the classroom. They could even dub over a video of an actual game.

?

Good goalies come and go, but which goalie has the highest winning percentage in NHL history?

Ken Dryden, with a .758 record.

As sports broadcasters often speak in short, choppy sentences, reluctant writers will not balk at putting pen to this type of dialogue. Surprising sound effects might just happen in the background.

Strategy—Call It Like It Is!

To motivate students to write more, encourage them to describe the action in a sport. For example, show a video of a snowboarder jumping off a snowy cliff or doing the moguls in a competition. Ask: What words would you use to describe the action? What was he/she doing? How would you describe the style of the snowboarder? In a competition, what makes for a high-scoring run?

This strategy could also be used with a skateboarding demonstration put on by class members or older students. Challenge the students to describe what they are doing. List the terminologies being used.

Strategy—Five Ways to Improve Your Game

Encourage Info-Kids to watch a news clip summary of a baseball, basketball, hockey, soccer or lacrosse game, showing all the highlights. As they watch the clip, challenge the students to make a list of how others could improve their game by studying the techniques shown. Sports enthusiasts may want to view and review the action in slow motion with the commentary turned off. Intense concentration will reveal the strategies and skills involved in clever moves. This activity could also be done using swimming and diving videos. A further refinement might be to locate "how-to" sports videos designed to improve the skill level of players or athletes.

If your Info-Kids like soccer, we recommend they enjoy Bob Mackin's dynamic *Soccer: The Winning Way*. Action photos of soccer greats, including Christian Vieri, Ronaldo, Batigol, Marcel Desailly, Davor Suker, Mia Hamm and Sun Wen, are interspersed with close-ups of boys and girls demonstrating soccer skills. The book has excellent text-photo correlation, with additional tips for focus. This is a high interest approach. Invite your students to check out some of the other "team sport" titles offered on the next page.

Focus on Resources

Sports Books Score Big

Get it straight! Finding out about yesterday's game is *not* reading! Info-Kids with a sports bent naturally gravitate to a greater diversity of reading material than do others. They are tuned into the daily newspaper section, regularly check out sports magazines, and will surf the Internet for the latest action, as well as information on their favorite teams, players and athletes. They want to be up to date and have the latest figures. Mind you, for relaxation, these Info-Kids may even extend themselves to browsing in encyclopedias of a sport, reading individual biographies of their heroes or watching out for books that will improve their own techniques.

There is a sports style of writing, slightly different from the television commentator style, that is fast-paced, filled with jargon of the game or sport, expressive, written in short sentences and action-focused. Resources written in this style are worth looking for to motivate outward-focused Info-Kids to read more.

Ever try a stalefish? What is it?

A stalefish is what skateboarder Tony Hawk had for dinner one day. It subsequently became the name for an innovative skateboard grab.

I brought in Sports Illustrated magazines for the kids. One boy took some home. He said his grandma liked to look at them too.
Al, teacher

Favorite Baseball Titles

- *Baseball* (Eyewitness) by James Kelley

- *Home Run Heroes: Big Mac, Sammy & Junior* (DK Readers, Level 3) by James Buckley, Jr.

- *Strikeout Kings* (DK Readers, Level 4) by James Buckley, Jr.

- *Who Is Baseball's Greatest Hitter?* by Jeff Kisseloff

- *The Young Baseball Player: A Young Enthusiast's Guide to Baseball* by Ian Smyth

Favorite Basketball Titles

- *Meet the Chicago Bulls* by Brendan Hanrahan

- *Meet the Los Angeles Lakers* by Joe Layden

- *The NBA Book of Big and Little* by James Preller

Favorite Hockey Titles

- *Amazing Forwards* by James Duplacey

- *Champion NHL Defensemen* by James Duplacey

- *Explosive Hockey Trivia* by Don Weekes

- *Extreme Hockey Trivia* by Don Weekes

- *Goal Scoring* by Sean Rossiter

- *Great Goalies* by James Duplacey

- *The Hockey Book for Girls* by Stacy Wilson

- *Hockey for Kids: Heroes, Tips and Facts* by Brian McFarlane

- *NHL Best Shots*

- *Rockin' Hockey Trivia* by Don Weekes

- *Top Rookies* by James Duplacey

Favorite Soccer Titles

- *Ball Control* by Gil Harvey

- *Soccer in Action* by Niki Walker and Sarah Dann

- *Soccer: The Winning Way* by Bob Mackin

Strategy—Climb to the Sky

Rock climbing has become a major sport for many adults on local cliffs and mountains. Rock climbing walls are put up at fairs and exhibitions for kids to try. One adventurous teacher, a climber herself, got her students totally involved in the novel she was reading aloud (*Banner in the Sky* by James Ullman) by bringing all her climbing gear to class. She also brought in a host of her favorite titles for the students to consult and to help figure out her equipment as they followed the climb in the novel.

Later, to entice them further, she arranged for them to visit a local sports centre that had a climbing wall. Many aching muscles later, the students were keen to find out more about how to go rock climbing for real. She used the magazine *Go Climb! 2001 Edition* for its glossy photos and dramatic action shots. She also encouraged the students to visit the Web site www.rockandice.com and to consult the following books:

- Benger, Michael, and Duane Raleigh. *Climbing Rock: Tools and Techniques.* This is the rock climbers' A to Z.
- Graydon, Don, and Kurt Hanson. *Mountaineering: The Freedom of the Hills* (6th ed.). Considered by many to be the bible of the sport, giving all the requisite fundamentals.
- Roberts, Jeremy. *Rock and Ice Climbing! Top the Tower* (Extreme Sports). Equipment, gear and beginning techniques.

Strategy—Going to the Extreme

Rock climbing appeals to some Info-Kids, but there are extreme sports books that will attract and excite other types of enthusiasts too. These include the following:

- Hawk, Tony, with Sean Mortimer. *Hawk. Occupation: Skateboarder.* Autobiography of one of the sport's greatest stars lets you know what life was really like off the ramp.
- Hayhurst, Chris. *Snowboarding! Shred the Powder* (Extreme Sports). How to get started in this popular sport.
- King, Andy. *Mountain Biking* (Play by Play). How to do it successfully. Also *Baseball* and *Hockey* in the series.
- Knotts, Bob. *Martial Arts* (A True Book). An overview of the different kinds of forms and goals, plus a glossary. Others in the series include *Cycling, Equestrian Events, Weightlifting* and *Wrestling.*
- Platt, Richard. *Extreme Sports* (DK Readers, Level 3). Get involved in whitewater rafting, inline skating, freestyle motorcycling, and more ...
- Schlegel, Elfi, and Claire Ross Dunn. *The Gymnastic Book: A Young Person's Guide to Gymnastics.* Demonstrates skills and training needed to be a winner.
- Schlesinger, Willy and Max. *Scooter Mania!* "Safe, fun tricks and cool tips for today's hottest ride."
- Richard, Jon (ed.). *World Championship Wrestling: The Ultimate Guide.* The who's who and what's what of the ring.

Focus on Reading-Thinking Skills

Synthesizing through Summary

A great skill for any Info-Kid, regardless of age, is the ability to state succinctly what an article or speaker has to say about a topic. Being able to summarize is to be able to put details together to form an entity—synthesizing the parts into a new whole. The challenge is to try to reduce the information given to the essential ideas and facts and come up with words and phrases that categorize these facts.

Summarizing can be as simple as paraphrasing or as complex as finding the theme of a text. Other levels include finding main ideas, creating topic sentences or making a synopsis of an entire text.

Strategy—What Did You Say?

Divide students into pairs or trios and ask them to read a short article of four or five paragraphs that gives an overview of a topic. Encyclopedias, nonfiction textbooks or the Web are good sources. Try to avoid passages that categorize the information explicitly. If the passages have headings, take them out. After reading the selection, ask your students to list all the points of information they can remember.

Then, have them sort the information in the text into three or four major categories. Tell them to delete repeated information. Encourage students to think of blanket terms to replace lists of items or actions: for example, "clothing" instead of socks, shirts, pants, coats and gloves; or "raptor" instead of eagle, hawk or falcon.

Challenge the students to invent a topic sentence for each category, giving only important information. These can be written on the chalkboard and ordered in an appropriate sequence. Other student groups can then read the sentences to check for extraneous information. Showing their editing by crossing out rather than erasing makes the process more concrete for reluctant readers.

The aim of this strategy is improve the students' ability to summarize information they read.

Strategy—Challenge the Title

The title can tell all! Divide students into pairs or small groups. Begin by reviewing that a good title is a phrase condensing the content of a passage. After reading a short passage, ask each group to discuss possible titles and, finally, to choose one.

The class can then review the titles and decide if each title describes the passage adequately. Consensus requires discussion until all agree on which are the most descriptive and accurate titles. After the decision is made, the whole group can discuss the criteria for judging a good title.

The aim of this strategy is to summarize the theme, gist or essence of the passage in clear, yet specific and descriptive language, and to become aware of criteria to use when creating titles.

Focus on Research-Project Skills

Defining the Topic Is the Goal

In any team sport, players know that they have to concentrate on the goal crease if they are to be successful in scoring. The same is true for a research project, only the concentration must begin immediately. The most important first step of any research endeavor is to answer the question "What do you want to know?" The answer to this becomes your topic, and identifies the theme and main points.

Choosing a topic for research is an important skill. Often the topic will be too large, too general or too unapproachable. One way to begin is by noting all aspects of a topic before deciding on a specific aspect. If done verbally with a teacher or parent, it is more fun because the stigma of having to write is removed. It is during this open-ended discussion period that new ideas are drawn out. It is a type of brainstorming. The world of horses, for example, is an enormous topic that includes breeds, raising young, care, history, racing, jumping and show horses, to mention but a few areas. Once an assortment of ideas are written down, encourage students to articulate exactly what aspect they want to find out about and what they do not. At this point, they need to pose the research questions they want to answer. Remember—we need to know what we want to know!

After developing an idea of the topic, students must pick out the important terms to use to support their search of the available information sources. Suppose, for example, that an animal lover is determined to research grizzly bears. Whether searching in an encyclopedia, reference book, library catalogue, or on the Internet, students will come up with a variety of related terms. They need to be reminded that a general-to-specific search is often the most productive. Hence, from mammals to bears to grizzly bears—or on another topic, from natural phenomena to weather to storms to tornadoes— can yield the best results. This type of search, from general term to more specific, is based on a logical combining of words similar to the Boolean system used to retrieve information in a computer database. Being able to find the general terms that can lead to more choices of places to find specific terms expands kids' researching abilities.

The point is to assist students to find and then define their topic for research. They need to realize that a variety of descriptors can get them to the information and help guide them through all the available information.

> Interviews with 12 dyslexics, including a Nobel laureate, a member of the US National Academy of Sciences, and other professionals in fields requiring reading, reveal all developed basic fluency three to four years later than peers, but still acquired Stage 5 skills (Chall's highest level of reading development) through avid reading about a topic of passionate interest.
>
> *Rosalie Fink,*
> *reading researcher*

Strategy—Zines Are In!

Invite the students to select a topic of current interest in the class and to design a magazine to feature it. Using a computer program will allow an impressive-looking product to emerge. The magazine could be topic specific, such as an issue on snowboarding or skateboarding, or it could be a general issue, such as one about different sports. Whatever they choose, encourage the students to remain focused on what they want to find out about. Francesca Block's *Zine Scene: Do It Yourself Guide to Zines,* which describes how to create and publish your own magazine, can help your students get started.

A struggling reader became successful once his father started bringing home comic books. The boy was proud of his progress and he began to bring that confidence into the classroom.

Jennette, teacher

Teacher Realities

Many outward-focused Info-Kids are boys who are fact- rather than fiction-oriented. Often throughout their elementary school years, they are faced with female teachers who prefer fiction. Male teachers, who often are more interested in information, have the advantage with these kids. Knowing this, it is imperative for female teachers to recognize and then cultivate any budding information interests of their own so that they have a basis for understanding Info-Kids' interests and can be on firmer ground for understanding Info-Kids. Remember to bring the influence of outward-focused fathers and other information gatherers and their "real world" interests into the classroom.

CHAPTER 7

Info-Kids Who Love Facts

Did you know that ... ?!

Characteristics
- Focus on single facts
- Pick out parts and pieces
- Love random trivia
- Amass collections

Resources for Success
- References and almanacs
- Trivia type books
- CD-ROM encyclopedias
- Specific Web sites
- Topic survey books
- Collection books

Many Info-Kids love to focus on facts because they like minutiae. Fact finders are of two kinds—the splitters and the lumpers. Splitters concentrate on one specific area of interest and lumpers on random miscellaneous facts for their own sake. Lumpers have a broad spectrum of interests and can turn out to be collectors of such items as mini cars, action figures or the ever-popular trading cards. They can also easily drop one interest in favor of another. In this they differ from the splitters, who concentrate on one interest in depth, perhaps for the rest of their life.

While Info-Kids who love facts are excellent at analyzing, which means they are good at picking out details within a topic, they are not very good at associating—making the connections among those details into any kind of order. They don't see the connection of one detail to another, how these details are related, or which details are important and which are extraneous. For example, they may know all the facts about the current hockey season, but might have difficulty connecting and categorizing similar facts about several hockey stars or teams. They live in a morass of details.

When reference is made to topics that will excite Info-Kids, certain classic obsessions keep turning up—specifically: dinosaurs, space and horses. A particular obsession may continue throughout their schooling and for the rest of their lives, or die within the school year and have its place taken by some other obsession next week or next year.

Meet the Info-Kids

Dalton—A Classic Passion

Energetic and intense, Dalton is obsessed with dinosaurs! Whenever he thinks the teacher has a free moment, he'll say, "I have to tell you something." His eyes shine and a smile breaks across his face when he has someone to listen to his ideas. He is a walking encyclopedia of dinosaur information and he thinks in analogies. While playing with a rubber ball in the gym, he says, "I like to jump on it like a velociraptor," or in art class when he has plastic potatoes on a plate, he refers to them as dinosaur eggs.

While other kids play during recess, he often draws beautifully proportioned, finely-detailed dinos along the sidewalk with chalk. He chooses the biggest and heaviest dinosaur books on the library shelf. During reading break, he always has a dino book and takes one home every night. Nothing else interests him!

Favorite Horses Titles
- *Horse: A Visual Guide to Over 100 Horse Breeds from around the World* by Elwyn Hartley Edwards
- *Horses* by Jackie Budd
- *Horses* by Tammy Everts and Bobbie Kalman
- *My Pony* by Louise Pritchard

Caitlin—Dreams Can Come True

Caitlin is a student who definitely has a preference for one topic. Her passion is horses. She started wanting to borrow only books about horses several years ago. When her teacher realized she could not steer her toward anything else, she went with the horses.

Over several years Caitlin has read everything in the library, both fiction and nonfiction, several times. She regularly goes to the public library to read books they have. She discovered the *Pony Pals* and *Stablemates* series. Whenever she has to do a report or a science fair project, she makes it have something to do with horses. Once she did research on the various breeds of horses. She even entered the school's speech festival to talk about horses. Finally, her dream came true. In grade seven she got her own horse!

Focus on Interests

In and Out of the Maze of Interests

Prepare to be overwhelmed by and amazed at the diversity of topics in which Info-Kids can become absorbed. There is no telling where their fact journeys will take them, how long they will pause on any topic, or what intensity will occur. Some may last a day, some a lifetime.

Strategy—Guest Experts

Info-Kids who have developed a great passion for a certain topic and who have a great deal of knowledge about it make wonderful "in-house" guest speakers. Teacher-librarians, realizing that their mandate is to have knowledge of all the resources of the school, both physical and human, need to uncover the talent among the students, teachers, staff and parents. It is their challenge to find out the interests, hobbies and special abilities of all who work in the school. How exciting it is for a primary youngster to be invited to a grade seven class to talk about dinosaurs, or for a grade seven boy who has champion dogs to talk to other classes about the training of dogs.

The value for these Info-Kids is the positive experience of being able to share their passions, but also in gaining valuable presentation skills. Time spent with these students in preparing their talks will pay off handsomely later.

Guest Experts
- Stamp and coin collectors
- Instrumentalists
- Computer enthusiasts
- Paleontologists
- Museum curators
- Television news reporters

Strategy—Create Your Own

There is no doubt about it, but many Info-Kids like to collect sports cards. Why not branch out and encourage them to create author cards, animal cards, extreme sports cards, etc.—in other words, cards based on their own particular interest(s). They can design these cards, based on ones they already have. If they create them on the computer, they can even publish them.

Focus on Resources

I Want the Facts

Many Info-Kids are fascinated with information and want to get quickly to the facts on a topic they are researching. As teachers we need to be astute in the selection of books we have in the classroom and the school library resource centre.

The format of such materials is crucial. For example, can students find the information they need efficiently? By this we are talking about a book having a visible organization which appears logical to the reader and is clear in its set-up. Are there headings which help to direct the reader? Most significantly, is there an index? If not—don't buy the book! We don't have money to waste on poorly formatted materials. Some resources without an index, however, are meant for browsing, and in their way serve a purpose as the random discovery of facts can lead Info-Kids to better structured and referenced resources. A table of contents is yet another tool that can assist Info-Kids in deciding if books have potential for their projects.

Favorite Ready References

- *Canadian Global Almanac*
- *Guinness Book of Records (Guinness World Records 2002)*
- *The Illustrated Dictionary of Classic Cars* by Graham Robson
- *Incredible Comparisons* by Russell Ash
- *Norris McWhirter's Book of Historical Records* by Norris McWhirter
- *The Oxford Children's Encyclopedia of Our World*
- *The Oxford Children's Encyclopedia of Science & Technology*
- *Scholastic Book of World Records 2002* by Jenifer Corr Morse
- *Visual Encyclopedia of Animals*
- *The World Almanac and Book of Facts 2002*
- *The World Almanac for Kids 2002*
- *The World Encyclopedia of Flags* by Alfred Znamierowski

Strategy—Facts Beyond Belief

What Info-Kids who love facts want and need are the facts. Great sources include the following:

- Angliss, Sarah. *Science Now.* Essential information in a coil-bound compendium.
- Ash, Russell. *The Top 10 of Everything.* It's all about awesome natural wonders and human achievements.
- Ash, Russell. *Top 10 Quiz Book.* Readers won't be able to resist these facts or trivia.
- Brown, Gerry, and Michael Morrison, eds. *The 2001 ESPN Information Please Sports Almanac.* What did happen in the 1999-2000 sports year?
- *The Handy Science Answer Book* (2nd ed.). Compiled by the Science and Technology Department of the Carnegie Library of Pittsburg. Answers ques-

Many reluctant readers take out nonfiction books precisely because they don't want anything that requires "consecutive" reading. They look at the pictures, maybe read the captions, and possibly bits of the text.

John, teacher

?

How long have we been told, "Remember to flush!"? When and by whom was the first flush toilet invented?

In 1778 by Joseph Bramah, who also invented the lock.

tions about physics, space, environment, biology, communications and the earth.

- Hare, Tony. *Animal Fact File: Head-to-Head Profiles of More Than 90 Mammals.* Full-page spreads on each mammal with specific features of its body, its skeleton and an intriguing fact column.
- Meikle, Marg. *Funny You Should Ask: Weird but True Answers to 115 1/2 Wacky Questions.* It's time to consider strange things about your body, clothes, food, sports, time and superstitions.
- Meikle, Marg. *You Asked for It! Strange but True Answers to 99 Wacky Questions.* Careful—you'll get caught reading the whole book!
- Morse, Jenifer Corr. *Scholastic Book of World Records 2002.* Bright, glossy blurbs feature outstanding accomplishments in nature, human-made items, science and technology, sport and popular culture. Clever use of graphs.
- Rogers, Kirsteen, et al. *The Usborne Internet-Linked Science Encyclopedia with 1,000 Recommended Web Sites.* A guide for searching cyberspace wisely.
- Yorke, Jane. *The Big Book of Trains: The Biggest, Fastest, Longest Locomotives on Rails.* Accurate facts and photographs of the history of trains and rail locomotion.

And, finally, a factual book with a different twist looks at how everyday things came into being. Don Wulffson's *The Kid Who Invented the Trampoline: More Surprising Stories about Inventions* looks at how in the world we got armor, blood transfusions, false teeth, ketchup, parking metres, surfboards, vending machines and the Zamboni.

Strategy—Facts Are for Sharing

The most important strategy a teacher or teacher-librarian can use with Info-Kids is to read sections of intriguing nonfiction books aloud. It could be as little as two or three sentences or a couple of paragraphs, a chapter, or, indeed, the entire book. Info-Kids won't let you read in a novel-like fashion, on and on … so you have to devise a new way to read aloud. They want to ask questions or comment on the information that is either given directly or inferred. They have a need to be stimulated with what is happening and to be challenged to give an opinion. Perhaps they don't realize this just quite yet, but they will in due time. As you read aloud to the class, diversify the strategies that you use to elicit an informational response. Remember to focus on the facts. Mind you, once you get into the story part, they will be hooked.

Some books, even though written as nonfiction, have a strong narrative quality to them. Frequently written in paragraph format with no headings to point out important information nor an index for easy retrieval of information, they prove a challenge for Info-Kids to access. What is exciting is that many of them have wonderful tales to tell of exciting happenings in our world. Try sharing some of the following:

- Montgomery, Sy. *The Man-Eating Tigers of Sundarbans.* Montgomery has a remarkable way of telling about her topic … as if she were sitting in front of us and chatting about it. This book, with its magnificent photographs, will hold Info-Kids spellbound. It makes us aware of the secret of the tigers in the mangrove swamp along the Bay of Bengal in southeastern India. Montgomery shares facts galore, so students will have to do an Info-Record as they listen

Kids with reading problems, usually boys, often want to take out books far beyond their reading level. Don't worry. Mom will help.

Anne, teacher

Topping Mt. Everest is still one of the extreme challenges. How many people reached the summit in 1993?

A real "peak" year—129 people accomplished this feat in 1993.

—to determine what she has shared in each part of the adventure—to keep track of them. Why are the tigers there? How do they survive? How does one find out about hidden truths?

- Montgomery, Sy. *The Snake Scientist.* Here's an engrossing account of a man studying tens of thousands of red-sided garter snakes in Manitoba. Each spring they come out of hibernation, meet to mate, and cover the landscape. Nic Bishop's amazing photos feature thousands of intertwined snakes.
- Simon, Seymour. *Destination: Jupiter.* The book uses current photos to highlight this exploration of a planet and its moons.
- Skreslet, Laurie, with Elizabeth MacLeod. *To the Top of Everest.* Highlights of a successful expedition to climb the world's most famous mountain. Photos feature action enroute to the top. This book could effectively be compared to Rebecca Stephens's new Eyewitness book *Everest,* which is a visual compendium of facts, customs, traditions, magnificent views and challenging physical settings.
- Tanaka, Shelley. *Discover the Iceman.* Accidentally discovered in 1991, the Iceman lived 4000 years ago. Here is the tale of the discovery, plus a fictional life story which pulls information from the past and gives it relevance for us today.

Strategy—Dino Delights

Dino fact finders would enjoy examining the following titles:

- Arnold, Caroline. *Giant Shark: Megalodon, Prehistoric Super Predator.* Look into the jaws of the largest predatory shark ever to live—some 2 million years ago.
- Barrett, Paul. *Dinosaurs.* More than 50 dinosaur profiles, range maps, size charts and detailed discriptions by a dinosaur expert outline the current ideas about these giants and their history.
- *BBC Walking with Dinosaurs: 3D Dinosaurs.* Just put on the glasses and watch these beasts come alive during four time periods.
- Brochu, Christopher, et al. *Dinosaurs* (The Time-Life Guides). An authoritative complex guide to dinosaurs, famous fossil sites and museums.
- *Dinosaur* (Eye Wonder). Vital information on the tough tactics of these prehistoric beasts.
- Haywood, Rosie. *The Great Dinosaur Search.* Captivating puzzles—find the dinos in small photos illustrated around the borders.
- Keiran, Monique. *Albertosaurus: Death of a Predator* (Discoveries in Paleontology). A snapshot of the life and times of one dinosaur preserved in the badlands of southern Alberta.
- Lambert, David. *DK Guide to Dinosaurs: A Thrilling Journey through Prehistoric Times.* Realistic models set in photos of natural settings.
- Madgwick, Wendy. *Questions and Answers: Dinosaurs.* Great answers to unusually challenging inquiries. More than 50 dinosaur profiles, range maps, size charts and detailed descriptions by an expert.
- Tanaka, Shelley. *Graveyards of the Dinosaurs.* Hunting for dinosaurs in Mongolia, Alberta and Argentina.

You have been transported back in time and come face to face with one of the hadrosaurs. Will he attack you or munch on the plant you're standing beside?

You're in luck. The hadrosaurs were plant eaters.

Finally, try Margaret Munro's *The Story of Life on Earth* to put the dinosaur eras in perspective in relation to other lives and times. Or, try Philip Ardagh's *Did*

Dinosaurs Snore? 100 ½ Questions about Dinosaurs Answered. These questions never asked and answered before will keep dinosaur keeners on their toes.

Focus on Reading-Thinking Skills

Associating

When students are associating they are making the connections between two things. In reading, as in thinking, the connection may be at the meaning, language structure or graphophonic level. It may be between a word and its meaning, a letter and its sound, an item and its category, the voice of two authors, or the units of an analogy. For example, Dalton, whom you met earlier, has a talent for seeing analogies between his favorite dinosaurs and his everyday world.

Strategy—What Is It?

Info-Kids love activities in which they have to solve a mystery. A simple set of clues challenges students to make associations in the process of guessing an object. Start by writing two words—clues—on the chalkboard or on a sheet of paper. Ask, "What do you think these words might be about?" Continue to present pairs of clues until six to ten are given or the students have guessed the object. For example: depth, underwater, ocean, dive, bow, radar, torpedoes ... submarine!

Discuss with the students their process of thinking through to the wanted word along with the kinds of associations made. The thinking behind the guesses can also be discussed. Such discussion helps students to understand the idea of associating and how to use it productively.

Strategy—Think of an Orange's Skin as the Earth's Crust

To help develop awareness of associating through analogies, start with a concept that is familiar and understood by your students, such as an orange, and then compare it to an unfamiliar concept, such as the physical makeup of the Earth. Far out? Not at all. Ask the students to list as many of the characteristics of an orange as possible. Their list might include: tough skin, sections, soft inside, seeds, juice, pulp, rind and zest. Then list the vocabulary related to the makeup of the Earth: inner core, crust, atmosphere, etc. The more characteristics you can produce for each of the two objects, the stronger the analogy.

Discuss which characteristics are similar—perhaps shape, structure, color, action, texture, smell, number, density or quality. This will help show that the orange's skin does appear to be like the Earth's crust in many ways. Students could use a Venn diagram to categorize the characteristics into similar and different ones, using one circle for the orange and the other for the Earth. Ask them to list the similarities in the overlapping segment of the two circles and the differences in the outside portions. Have students explain their reasoning in finding similarities and differences between the two concepts.

The point of this strategy is to explore possibilities; to discover how something unfamiliar is alike or different from something more familiar. Similes, metaphors, allegories and parables are all types of analogies.

All perception of truth is the perception of analogy; we reason from our hands to our head.
Henry David Thoreau,
American writer and philosopher

Strategy—Clean It or Shovel It!

One aspect of being able to make associations is being able to place items into appropriate groups. Let's start with the only place an Info-Kid can have his own privacy—the bedroom. Using index cards, adhesive notes, the chalkboard or the overhead, ask students to brainstorm everything that they have stashed away in the bedroom. Have students make a general list of items or arrange cards on the floor or table.

Afterward, ask students to identify how these might belong in a four-drawer dresser. For example:

- How could you group items together?
- Which drawer would you put them in? Why?
- What would you label each drawer to tell what was in it?
- For what reason do some things not belong in the drawers?
- Where might you put them?
- What can you label them?

When students are associating, they are making the connections between two things. This strategy can be used as a precursor to the selecting of categories for a research project. It helps in understanding the organization of a collection of facts.

Focus on Research-Project Skills

What Have I Got?

Organizing information is a challenge for most students when they undertake a fact-finding project. "How do I teach it?" is a frequent refrain heard by teachers. A card trick helps! Encourage students, when taking notes, to write each fact on a small recipe card, adhesive note or other scrap of paper. Then, have them spread the fact cards out on a table to see what they have. Finally, have the students move the papers around until there are clustered groups of facts they can categorize and label.

Being able to view all the facts separated out into groups across a tabletop will give students a chance to see what they have, if they have found enough information on the topic, or if there are gaps. The point of this strategy is to assist students in seeing how facts fit into categories and in being able to check their selection of categories for a research project.

Strategy—Starts and Finishes

Divide students into pairs or trios and give each a computer disk with the middle portion only of a report on a specific topic, perhaps the recent water pollution scares in small towns, or an endangered species. Give half of the groups the introduction as well, and the other half the conclusion. On their computers, have students read and comment on the major ideas of the report. Ask those who received the introduction to write an appropriate conclusion and the others a good introduction. After each group finishes a section, it can be compared to those of the other students and to the originals.

I've always been curious, and I love finding out new and amazing facts. One of the things that I like best about writing is gathering information for a new book. Researching is something like being on a treasure hunt with each new fact being a clue to where to look next.

Caroline Arnold, children's author quoted in Flora Wyatt

Use facts which impress students and share them the with the class by means of graphs, diagrams or maps. All of these are subtle ways of demonstrating the organization and classification of facts. You may wish to show the wing spans of large and small birds, the lengths of rivers, the speed of animals, cars, planes, etc.

Teacher Realities

Often Info-Kids will know more about a given topic than we do. Don't let that intimidate you. There is nothing wrong with not knowing everything—even as a teacher. It is far more important to recognize that these kids have knowledge, to value their expertise, to acknowledge it, and to promote it in class. Being the class expert means the student gets to guide the way and to lead the group. Expertise is power and anything that gives reluctant readers power in the classroom can be used to help overcome their reluctance or reading problems.

CHAPTER 8

Info-Kids Who Are Hands-On

Just let me do it!

Characteristics

- Take things apart
- Build things
- Are physically involved
- Manipulate materials

Resources for Success

- How-to-make-things books (e.g., models, pop-ups)
- Cooking and craft books
- Science experiments
- Instructional manuals
- How-to-draw books
- Calligraphy books
- Computers and the Internet

Some Info-Kids just have to keep busy. These "doers" use their hands extremely well and like to handle objects and make things. They are usually physically adept as their balance and small motor control are finely developed. They love anything that requires "doing." While fiddling around with objects, they want to know how things go together or come apart. Clocks, motors and the insides of machines prove to be most enticing.

In the classroom, these hands-on Info-Kids are constantly fiddling with something, becoming the doodlers and the paper folders. Activities such as building models, making crafts, playing sports, experimenting with science activities, cooking, and generally messing around, are their forte. Often these kids surprise us—while seemingly aimlessly doodling all day, they are the ones that then go home and build a hydrofoil or a model airplane. These are the kids who change our world, who grow up to be rocket scientists, engineers, general contractors and crafts people.

Meet the Info-Kids

Rajit—Champion Surfer

Rajit is obsessed with computers. Every lunch hour he is off to the computer lab to play around on the Internet or explore other programs. With a computer in his room at home, where he is literally glued to the screen most evenings, he sees his absorption with computers as an "in" with his peers. Rajit spends his allowance in buying computer magazines, which he reads avidly in order to keep up with the latest developments. This allows him during daily sharing time to elaborate on the latest information he has found on new computer models and their specifications. He always uses computer lingo with his peers.

What is exciting is that Rajit learns by trying things out, playing on the keyboard and experimenting in a playful mood, rather than being overly impressed by the technology. Frequently he discovers what others don't know and always seems to know a short cut for accomplishing a task on the computer. He is very open about his ability and always willing to help others with computer strategies.

Matt—Iron Chef!

Matt only wants to borrow cookbooks, a commodity not found much in school libraries. He will take a novel, but it is questionable if he cracks it open before returning it without comment.

Matt is taking a cooking course and is fascinated with recipes. He collects them and actually makes something everyday. Favorites at the moment are cinnamon pinwheels, peanut butter and jam muffins, an assortment of cookies, and the ever-popular pizza crust from scratch! Matt also watches cooking shows and tries out some of the recipes on his brothers. He even creates his own concoctions. He has written the ones he likes in his own "cookbook."

Focus on Interests

I Want to Do It!

Every generation has its builders and destroyers. Info-Kids who are hands-on are the builders in life. These tactile and kinesthetic learners are keenly intrigued with the "doing," processing knowledge by handling it. They search out manuals, handbooks and instruction sheets to guide them through their manipulations. Just as with Info-Kids who love facts, the range of interests can be quite phenomenal, touching on everything that people "do." The more intense the involvement, the greater will be the fascination, and vice versa.

Favorite Cross-Section Books

- *The Coolest Cross-Sections Ever* by Richard Platt
- *Inside the Whale and Other Animals* by Ted Dewin
- *Look Inside Cross-Sections: Rescue Vehicles* by Louisa Somerville
- *Nature Cross-Sections* by Richard Orr
- *Star Wars: Incredible Cross-Sections* by David West Reynolds
- *Steven Biesty's Cross-Sections: Castle* by Richard Platt
- *Steven Biesty's Incredible Explosions: Exploded Views of Astonishing Things* by Richard Platt

---

Strategy—Surfing the Internet

It is totally mind boggling to think of just how much information is on the Internet and how much is being added even as you read these words. Surfing has become a very popular pastime and is one that takes time and talent to devise successful strategies.

To be successful, we must chose a search engine that will meet our needs. Many Info-Kids have found *Google,* a favorite with adults because it gets relevant things quickly. This search engine's main feature is its relevancy ranking system. Another important feature is that words put between quotation marks are considered as a phrase. In other words, it automatically puts a plus designation between words. Other engines do not do this. For example, you can use phrases such as "fish aquarium," "police Canadian" or "volcanoes Iceland" to

You're really going to put onion in that sandwich? What's the best kind to use?

A red onion has a sweeter and milder taste than most onions.

get what you want. Give students time to explore various search engines and to compare their strengths and weaknesses.

Strategy—Creative Cooking without Cookbooks?

Info-Kids cook without a cookbook? Of course, they can creatively surf the Web and get lost in thousands of recipes. Our friend John wanted to cook a Jamaican dinner for his family, so, using Google as the search engine, he typed in "Jamaican salad" and got a vast array from which to choose. It turned out to be a delicious choice.

The Iron Chef—www.ironchef.com—has a great following among youngsters. Try this unofficial site for a delicious entry into the world of culinary art. Need some more recipes? Try www.allrecipes.com.

Strategy—Bake Off!

Many students like to cook, and boys need to be reminded that many of the great chefs in the world are men. Using a computer program to format it, why not have the students create a class recipe book? It could be a collection of everyone's favorites, easy-to-make after-school snacks, quick breakfast treats, or any other suggested theme.

Focus on Resources

How-to-Make and Hands-On Books

Is it any surprise that many Info-Kids who are hands-on are actively involved in projects? They like to make things, and, fortunately for them, there are an impressive number of books available. Some are better than others. What to watch for? Sequential descriptions, step-by-step directions, clarity of illustrations, preciseness of text and clear images of the final product are musts. We must be selective in our choice of such how-to-make books. Ones with fuzzy illustrations and unclear instructions should not be bought or should be discarded.

The second type of hands-on resource has special effects that can be manipulated in the books themselves: for example, flaps, plastic overlays, pop-ups or 3-D glasses. These features often lead to doing things, particularly in the science and art titles. Suggested experiments in such books prove to be popular with many Info-Kids.

Strategy—How to Make?

Here are some excellent resources for those Info-Kids who just have to make things:

- Biddle, Steve and Migumi. *Planet Origami: Cosmic Paper Folding for Kids.* Aliens, spaceships, astronauts and shooting stars—all for the folding.
- Blackburn, Ken, with designs by Den Blackburn and Jeff Lammers. *The World Record Paper Airplane Book.* Besides background information on the

---

What makes a soda "pop"?

The carbonated water with which it is made.

Favorite Cookbooks
- *American Heart Association Kids' Cookbook* edited by Mary Winston
- *Just Desserts and Other Treats for Kids to Make* by Marilyn Linton
- *KidsCooking: A Very Slightly Messy Manual* edited by Klutz
- *Kids in the Kitchen: 100 Delicious, Fun and Healthy Recipes to Cook and Bake* by Micah Pulleyn and Sarah Bracken
- *Roald Dahl's Revolting Recipes* by Josie and Felicity Fison

principles of flight and throwing techniques, this book includes 16 model designs, 10 ready-to-fold planes and a runway.

- Diehn, Gwen. *Making Books That Fly, Fold, Wrap, Hide, Pop up, Twist and Turn.* The how-to of over a dozen book types, plus history and hints on making them.
- Folder, Alan. *Paper Tricks.* Tricks and games to fold from paper with easy step-by-step directions. Dazzling paper included.
- Kelly, Sarah. *Amazing Mosaics.* Clear images and instructions for using paper, shells and seeds to create mosaic picture frames, bookmarks, boxes and more.
- Lacey, Sue. *Start with Art: Animals.* Paws, ears, snouts, fur and skin—all different, but all become graphically clear following the easy directions.
- Lacey, Sue. *Start with Art: People.* The human figure is not as difficult as it looks. Sketch your favorite for practice.
- Schmidt, Norman. *Best Ever Paper Airplanes.* Be flight smart with these basic construction folds and plans for 18 stellar airplanes.
- *Squashing Flowers, Squeezing Leaves: A Nature Press and Book.* Includes an easy-to-use press, full instructions for drying, plus ideas for using the dried products.
- *The Ultimate Lego Book.* A guide to the world of Lego, its history and achievements, models and how-to hints.

Favorite How-to Books

- *The Amazing Book of Paper Boats* by Jerry Roberts
- *The Cootie Catcher Book* edited by Klutz
- *Electric Gadgets and Gizmos: Battery-Powered Buildable Gadgets That Go!* by Alan Bartholomew
- *Make Amazing Toy and Game Gadgets* by Amy Pinchuik
- *Make Cool Gadgets for Your Room* by Amy Pinchuik
- *Ultimate Robot Kit* edited by Dorling Kindersley

Strategy—How to Do?

Info-Kids who are hands-on often need the stimulus of a challenge to get them into reading. Bring in an armload of books and let them browse through them until they find something that interests them. It could be a feat of magic, a way of drawing horses, or directions on how to tie knots. Here are a few resources to get your students started:

- Burke, Judy. *Look What You Can Make with Paper Bags.* A multitude of ideas with step-by-step instructions to make costumes, dolls, beads, pencil holders and puppets from paper bags.
- Cassidy, John. *The Klutz Book of Knots.* A well-illustrated, step-by-step guide to 24 useful knots, with rope and holes attached.
- Cassidy, John, and Michael Stroud. *The Klutz Book of Magic.* Want to be amazing and amaze others? 31 tricks and 5 props.
- Cobb, Vicki. *Magic ... Naturally! Science Entertainments & Amusements* (rev. ed.). Impress your friends and family.
- MacLeod, Elizabeth. *Get Started Stamp Collecting for Canadian Kids.* Where to find stamps and equipment, and what the pros look for.

Strategy—Catch the Wind

It is a proven belief of seasoned teachers that windy days result in restless students and an urge to get out and fly. Info-Kids will be delighted to be challenged to go outside and fly a kite! Such literal instructions will bring out the best in them, especially if they have to make their own kites for a flying contest. Almost immediately, kite-making manuals will be consulted, and parents may become more involved than they would like ... but all will be well if dads and moms are allowed in the competition too!

While students are actively devising plans to build kites, research could be done on kites around the world. For example: Kites in history— Where were these "wind gods" used and why? Kites as spies—Who used them? Kite fighting—How do Japanese, Chinese and North American kites compare? What are the differences when comparing size, shape and personality?

Besides this, Info-Kids will need to seek out techniques for flying kites—both preparing for the launch and successful flying. How does one use the wind most efficiently? What role does the wind play?

Encourage your students to consult one of the following titles for great ideas:

- Dixon, Norma. *Kites: Twelve Easy-to-Make High Fliers.* Beginners' fun.
- Michael, David. *Step-by-Step Making Kites.* Simple directions for making and flying nine types of kites.
- Stevens, Beth Dvergsten. *Colorful Kites.* Historical toys? A great introduction, along with tips on building, flying and safety. Includes excellent, trouble-shooting tips for correcting flying problems.

Strategy—Finding Quality Internet Sites

The American Library Association has a wonderful service available. On its Web site, it posts the results of a committee of librarians who have researched quality Internet locations. It is called *700+ Great Sites!* and can be found at www.ala.org/parentspage/greatsites/amazing.html.

We asked our Info-Kid friend, John, to have fun with about 50 of the sites. His recommendations include the following:

- www.astr.ua.ed/4000WS.html
  4,000 Years of Women in Science gives a great deal of information through biographies and photographs.
- www.batcon.org
  Bat Conservation International tells you what you need to know about bats.
- www.miamisci.org/hurricane/
  This site provides a lot of information about storms, weather instruments and, of course, hurricanes. There is a section for kids who have been in natural disasters to write about what has happened.
- www.gsrg.nmh.ac.uk/
  This well-designed site gives a shattering amount of information about earthquakes and the history of famous ones.
- http://volcano.und.nodak.edu/
  Volcano World features up-to-date information on current eruptions.
- www.nationalgeographic.com/cats/
  Cats Plans for Perfection has excellent graphics showing the biology of a cat step by step.

Encourage your Info-Kids to check out the main site, some of those listed above, and others that they may find. Challenge them to establish a rating scale for each site.

Focus on Reading-Thinking Skills

Synthesizing through Sequence

Sequence is about order. Events, episodes, directions and time all happen in a set sequence. A historical time line, a set of directions, or even a recipe is a form of sequence. Sequence in a text can be shown visually in many forms: for example, through charts, diagrams, stepped lines or circle lines. Certain connective words/phrases also signal sequence within a text, including words and phrases like: first, then, later, next, soon, tomorrow, yesterday, in the future, in the evening, next year and finally.

Strategy—What's the Connection?

What are the connecting words and phrases that we use to indicate sequences of different kinds? Begin by asking students to identify a few such word groups (e.g., first, second, last), then have students search for more in a social studies or science text. Later, have them try looking in a nonfiction trade book. Challenge students to develop a class chart of these and other sequence words/phrases they find elsewhere.

If looking for connecting words and phrases is too difficult for your students, begin by having them order concrete objects according to a particular criteria; for example, ordering pencils for length or apples for size. Encourage the students to name the sequence (e.g., first the red one, then the blue one, and last is yellow). Progress to having the students order pictures of parts of an event they observed over time.

Finally, have students order three sentences into a paraphrase that uses sequence-connecting words. For example, "He walked to school. He went by the fire station. He walked by the police station. He walked by the mini-mart" could be combined and sequenced as "When he walked to school, he first went by the fire station, then the police station, and finally the mini-mart." This sequence uses the sequencing words: "first," "then" and "finally."

Any of the above sequencing exercises can be made easier or more difficult by the number of objects, pictures or sentences included. The point of the strategy is to become aware of the connecting words/phrases that are used to indicate sequences of different kinds.

Strategy—Tell It Like It Is!

After a session on the Internet looking for information on a topic they are interested in, ask students to tell the group the sequence of their search. Direct them with questions such as:

- Which site did you start with?
- Where did you go next?
- Where did that send you to?

When students uncover and discover patterns and relationships themselves, they remember them.
Regie Routman,
educator and researcher

- Where could you have gone instead?
- What sequence gave the most useful information?

As they talk, chart their searches on the board. Encourage them to use connecting sequence words to help make their description make sense to their listeners.

The point of this strategy is to encourage students to use sequencing efficiently in their oral descriptions of their work, which, in turn, aids them in ordering their thoughts logically.

Focus on Research-Project Skills

Flesh Out the Skeleton

"I've got the facts ... I have them categorized ... What now?" All too often, students take the raw information and just start writing up the project, with no idea of its structure or organization. In actual fact, they forget about its skeleton —the logical structure within each category and, indeed, within the organization of the whole report.

The point of the strategies that follow is to assist the students in developing their organizational skills so that they are able to sequence the information they find in their research endeavors. Gaps in knowledge to be filled later may begin to show as these two sequences are developed.

Strategy—Sequencing Categories

To organize the structure of a category, get the students to lay out the cards or papers on which they have listed the facts they have assigned to that category on a table, so that they can see what information they have. The challenge is to examine the items to establish a sequence.

The question becomes: What is the best order within a group of facts? Some sequences might include:

- From most general to most specific
- By order of directions
- By a historical time line
- By what is known to that which is being speculated about

Flexibility in arranging the cards allows students to consider various means of sequencing the information within each category.

Strategy—Putting It All Together

The other sequence needed is that of arranging the categories of facts within the report as a whole. Students will need to use logic to decide: Which category should go first? Which next? And then? Finally? Again, thinking about the order of directions, time lines, general to specific items, or other possible sequences, will determine the best sequence.

I have found that some reluctant participants turn on when given hands-on projects such as making a diorama or drawing that supports a cooperative group's oral presentation effort.

Erin, teacher

Teacher Realities

For Info-Kids who are reluctant readers and tactile learners, we must provide a physical component with instruction. That means using whatever requires movement of some sort—anything that gets the physical body involved. The more ways we can find to use motion in instruction the better. Good options include various kinds of writing activities, dramatic role-play and tableaux, readers' theatre with actions, individual projects requiring creating artifacts as part of the final presentation, and the use of computers.

CHAPTER 9

Info-Kids Who Act Out or Hide Out

Who me? I'm not available!

Characteristics

- Become avoidance experts
- Communicate through behavior
- Exhibit hyperactivity
- Practise invisibility

Resources for Success

- Highly visual references
- DK Eyewitness books
- Internet
- Interactive books
- Game books

Because Info Kids who act out or hide out do not feel connected to classroom activities and are bored to tears, they become expert avoidance specialists. Their behavior is their communication. Rather than talk, they prefer to disrupt or disappear. Depending on their need for physical activity, they either make their presence felt or not.

The Info-Kids who act out are those who are exceptionally physically active. We see them pacing around the classroom, rocking in a chair, tapping pencils on a desk, or leaning over it in a gravity-defying feat. On the other hand, super passive Info-Kids are often found under desktops, behind bookcases, under tables or behind easels. Their minds, as well as their bodies, are hiding out, and in escaping to a safe retreat, they are saying, "I'm not available!" Unfortunately for their learning, we often accept their passive behavior and ignore them because they are not disruptive.

Meet the Info-Kids

Mick—Wow! It's a Red-belly Newt!

Mick is obsessed with the red-belly newt. For whatever reason, he finds them fascinating. Try as the teacher might to engage him in a group discussion on types of pets, Mick would not take this sitting down, and would actively try to convince others to change the topic to newts. He pasted papers on the board that said "red-belly newt" and regularly brought books to school that were about the topic.

The teacher was near her wit's end with this obsession, but finally she decided to go with his flow and helped him to find more information on newts. Then she challenged him to share the information that he had with the class. His interest turned into a wonderful project with a great presentation. Mick made full use of the visuals he found and the Internet sites and adult references he surveyed. He also became a popular guest newt expert in several other classes during the year.

Ernestine—Vladivostok or Bust!

Ernestine, a grade-five student, is small for her age and is content to be in her own world in the classroom. She quickly does her math assignments, actively does independent science projects, but steadfastly refuses to take part in the music program, the educational drama activities, and games in physical education. Fortunately for her, the teacher is patient and does not force her to participate, but does not allow any distracting behavior either.

Ernestine is accepted by her fellow students, but is not an active part of the group. When directly asked for her opinion, she reluctantly shares her ideas. She does, however, have a passion for geography—particularly place names. During an individualized spelling session, her partner panicked as he looked at her words: Novosibirsk, Petropavlovsk-Kamchotskiy, Irkutsk, Chelyabinsk. He couldn't even pronounce them, let alone spell them! Not a problem for Ernestine. She just wrote the Russian cities from memory!

When Ernestine's parents came for a parent-child conference with the teacher, they began by saying how much they appreciated all that the teacher had done for Ernestine. Mystified, the teacher was a little taken aback when they told him that at home Ernestine regularly gathered up all the younger children in the neighborhood and taught them the songs, games and story dramas that the rest of the class had done. Looking over at Ernestine, the teacher said, "Well, you fooled me, eh?" Smugly, she replied, "Yup!" One never knows what these hide-out Info-Kids are taking in.

Focus on Interests

Animals and Travel Have Universal Appeal

In practically any study focusing on student reading interest, animals place high on the list. From a very young age, kids have a love for beasties! After delighting in the familiar and fuzzy—rabbits, kittens and teddy bears—the strange and exotic have the appeal—slick and scaly, multi-legged, antennae-wielding, or massive and man-eating. Studying exotic animals can lead to studying their habitats, which in turn can lead to armchair traveling of new environments. In the end comes the allure of faraway places.

Strategy—All I Want for Christmas Is … !

Not every Info-Kid wants a newt for Christmas, nor should they, but all students need an opportunity to have a platform to indulge their interests. Why not a campaign to promote newts or another interesting creature or creatures? "Give your kid a newt!" or "Why Newts?"—posters, slogans, press releases and assemblies can be featured. An amusing debate might be held on a topic such as

---

Interesting Creature Titles

- *Animals Nobody Loves* by Seymour Simon
- *Dig Wait Listen: A Desert Toad's Tale* by April Sayre
- *Poison Dart Frogs* by Jennifer Dewey
- *The Really Wicked Droning Wasp and Other Things That Bite and Sting* by Theresa Greenaway
- *Reptiles and Amphibians* by David S. Kirshner

Favorite Bug Titles

- *The Best Book of Bugs* by Claire Llewellyn
- *Bug Faces* by Darlyne A. Murawski
- *Bugs: A Close-Up of the Insect World*
- *Creepy Crawlies* by Christina Coster-Longman
- *Discovery Channel Insects and Spiders*
- *Incredible Bugs: An Eye-Opening Guide to the Amazing World of Insects* by Rick Imes
- *Mealworms: Raise Them, Watch Them, See Them Change* by Adrienne Mason
- *Spiders* by Barbara Taylor
- *Spiders* by Kevin J. Holmes
- *Spiders and Their Web Sites* by Margery Facklam
- *What's That Bug? Everyday Insects and Their Really Cool Cousins* by Nan Froman

"Better Bet: Dogs vs Newts!" Have students consider how certain creatures are alike and what different appeals each has.

Strategy—Out of Africa

Info-Kids can be beasts at heart! Give them a chance to become their favorite one by challenging them to create a drama of a game hunter going to the African plains in search of game. Although the animals are all around him, he does not see them. Once students have selected what they want to become, challenge them to use nonfiction books to design a papier-maché mask and head piece in the shape of their chosen animal. The questions now become: How do the animals move? How do they walk? How do they survey the scene? This will lead to repeated viewings of videos of African animals.

Info-Kids will become absorbed with their animal and will note many details of movement. Why not find out other facts about them too? Decisions will have to be made about effective costumes—perhaps just colored tights with simple attachments will do. The remaining challenge will be the music. Will animals have their own theme selections? With the addition of music, the drama may become a dance drama. Sssh! Don't tell the boys too soon. Let them get hooked first.

Strategy—The Rain in Spain!

Is it raining? The popular song from *My Fair Lady* can lead us to explore weather conditions around the world. Simply putting in a head like "Anchorage weather" (with quote marks) or any other city will give several sources for the weather on the Internet—from national weather bureaus, to daily newspapers, to tourist information. Try city tourist bureaus to find out about forthcoming trips. One exciting feature of many sites is the "virtual tour" of hotels, cruise ships, and even submarines.

Favorite African Animal Titles

- *Elephants* by Barbara Taylor
- *Gorillas* by Seymour Simon
- *Great Apes* by Barbara Taylor
- *Lion* by Caroline Arnold
- *Rhino* by Caroline Arnold

What's wrong with your left arm, Dr. Livingstone?

Explorer Dr. David Livingstone was mauled by a lion in 1844.

Strategy—Escape!

We all have times in our lives when we would love to escape to an island. What better way to incorporate an Info-Kid into the mainstream of the classroom than to challenge each student in the class to research an island they would like to escape to. Be prepared—they won't all be hot destinations. Iceland and Greenland do have their attractions!

Encourage the students to see what they can find on the Internet, in almanacs and in reference books. Writing to tourist boards or embassies may produce some visual material for sharing in a presentation to the class. These projects can have the advantage of being done over a longer time frame, thus providing flexibility for Info-Kids.

Focus on Resources

Wow! Look at This!

Info-Kids often need to be hooked visually to get into relevant resources. They can become fascinated by particular wildlife, or photo essays or accounts of life cycles of animals, but they often need a great cover of a book or a flashy Web site to grab their attention. The same is true for those who are keen on traveling to faraway places—the photos must be intriguingly full of details. This is the reason why books similar to the Eyewitness series have become so popular and have resulted in a multitude of spin-offs.

Photographs should not be blurry renditions of objects shot at a distance. Info-Kids want close-up perspectives and sharp, crisp images. They like those such as Nic Bishop's in *Red-Eyed Tree Frog* by Joy Cowley. This eye-to-eye photo essay of the life of an adorable frog immediately captures their attention.

Drawings give a richness that photographs cannot. Good ones clarify the details, simplify the structure and point out the important aspects of objects. All of these qualities are evident, for example, in a quality bird guide.

Strategy—Animal Alert

We all need to know more about endangered species, or indeed any interesting animals other than the usual dogs and cats. Challenge Info-Kids to construct a Web site about a specific animal. After considering other Web sites, students can determine how they want to design the site, how to organize it, and what facts are important to include.

Many ideas can be found in the following references:

- Funston, Sylvia. *Animal Feelings* (the Secret Life Of Animals). Can animals be like humans?
- Hickman, Pamela. *Animal Senses: How Animals See, Hear, Taste, Smell and Feel*. Put the facts to work—nifty experiments to try.
- Hodge, Deborah. *Beavers, Deer, Moose, Elk and Caribou*. What is it like to be one of these famous mammals?
- Latimer, Jonathan, and Karen Nolting. *Songbirds* (Peterson Field Guides for Young Naturalists). A chorus of your favorite early morning soloists.
- Mattison, Chris. *Snake*. A herpetologist's delight.

Bad day! You've just crossed the path of a rubber boa. What are its measurements to tell your friends?

You just might be lucky. One of the smallest boas, the rubber boa, rarely grows over two feet.

?

Sharks get all the publicity! But what freshwater fish is credited with killing more people than the great white shark?

The South American piranha, which is less than a foot long.

- McMillan, Bruce. *Wild Flamingos.* Photo essay on the largest species of flamingos that live on the island of Bonaire.
- Swanson, Diane. *Feet That Suck and Feed* (Up Close). Feet can be useful for feeding, swimming, climbing, leaping and running on water!
- Swanson, Diane. *HeadGear That Hides and Plays* (Up Close). It's what is on top that counts! Simple introduction to the heads of several animals, birds and fish.
- Swinburne, Stephen R. *Bobcat: North America's Cat.* Don't try to cosy up to this critter.

However, should your students want to find out more about their dog, cat or other pet, invite them to try these resources:

- Farran, Christopher. *Animals to the Rescue! True Stories of Animal Heroes.* Twenty-six, action-packed and incredible stories of remarkable rescues and amazing animals.
- Fogle, Bruce. *The New Encyclopedia of the Dog.* Everything you ever wanted to know about every dog you might bring home.
- George, Jean Craighead. *How to Talk to Your Dog.* How to understand your dog and make him understand you.
- Gersten, Sheldon L., with Jacque Lynn Schaltz. *ASPCA Complete Guide to Dogs.* Explicit but readable "how-to" and "why" knowledge from the experts.
- Lauber, Patricia. *The True-or-False Book of Cats.* All about cat history, science, legends, talk and mysteries such as: Can cats see in total darkness? And, why do cats bring home their prey?

Strategy—Specialized Nature Books

Besides magnificent comprehensive books about the animal kingdom, many authors and photographers are attracted to one species, one location, or one problem in our wild world. Fortunately for their readers, these books have dramatic formats that invite lingering. Consider the following:

- Blum, Mark. *Galápagos in 3-D.* Breathtaking stereoscopic views of life on the islands.
- Cruxton, J. Bradley. *Discovering the Amazon Rainforest* (Discovery). Life in the Amazon—its people, nature, products and the troubled rainforest.
- Earle, Sylvia A. *Hello, Fish! Visiting the Coral Reef.* Captivating underwater shots of life in and around the reef.
- Kent, Peter. *Hidden under the Ground: The World beneath Your Feet.* Intricate drawings and fact-filled pages show what happens down under where trains run, pipes flow, animals burrow, gold is found and dungeons are used to imprison.
- Lessem, Don. *Inside the Amazing Amazon.* Various layers of the rainforest, from floor to canopy, come to life when fold-out pages reveal rich, detail-packed scenes. Numbered guide helps identification.
- Orr, Richard. *The Burrow Book.* All about animals and their burrowing habits in woodlands, deserts, forests, grasslands, and even the Arctic.
- *Rain Forest* (Eye Wonders). Who is it that calls the jungle home?
- Swanson, Diane. *Coyotes in the Crosswalk: Canadian Wildlife in the City.* Facts and figures on animals that seem to thrive in urban areas.

- Willis, Paul M. *Rocks and Minerals* (My First Pocket Guide). Basic source for amateur geologists.

Strategy—Armchair Travelers

Info-Kids with a flair for geography are often entranced by accounts of other people's travels. They love browsing, in their own unique way, in back issues of *National Geographic, World* and *Owl* magazines or in travel books. Although for reluctant readers it is usually the photographs that catch their attention, they will also wander to the captions and parts of the text. Frequently, travel accounts have a narrative quality to them, which lessens their appeal, but if an account is in a diary or journal format, attention is heightened. It is then the real thing about a real person.

Many books make for a wonderful read-aloud experience for both teachers and students. Some of these include:

- Aulenbach, Nancy, and Hazel Barton. *Exploring Caves: Journeys into the Earth.* Visit underground caves and the microscopic creatures that live in them from Greenland to Mexico with an IMAX film crew.
- Bowers, Vivien. *Wow Canada! Exploring This Land From Coast to Coast to Coast.* An exciting montage of photos, humorous drawings, maps, illustrations and short pieces of text.
- Coffey, Maria, with Debora Pearson. *My South Sea Adventure: Jungle Islands.* Experience paddling around the Pacific's Solomon Islands in a kayak through Dag Goering's remarkable photos.
- Hooper, Meredith. *Antarctic Adventure: Exploring the Frozen South* (DK Readers, Level 4). Six freezing journeys on this icy continent.
- Knight, Tim. *Journey into the Rainforest.* Knight's account of a visit to the Amazon is interspersed with dramatic photos and fascinating facts.
- Lourie, Peter. *The Mystery of the Maya: Uncovering the Lost City of Palenque.* Exploring the secrets of a forgotten society deep in the Mexican jungle.
- Raskin, Lawrie, with Debora Pearson. *My Sahara Adventure: 52 Days by Camel.* The romance of traveling desert sands without the grit or the heat! Raskin's exceptional photograph journey across the desert to Timbuktu gives insight into many aspects of Sahara life. What an experience!
- Turnbull, Andy, with Debora Pearson. *By Truck to the North.* Travel from the freeways of Vancouver to the ice roads of the north. The destination? Tuktoyaktuk. Turnbull takes us as co-adventurers through the Rockies and up the Alaska Highway to deliver groceries above the Arctic Circle.

Focus on Reading-Thinking Skills

Predicting

Predicting is educated guessing—creating a hypothesis. The point of predicting is to speculate about the future, to consider where the facts you have at hand could go, or to create a theory about something.

To predict consequences, explain unfamiliar phenomena or hypothesize, a student needs to be able to answer the question: "What would happen if ...?" To explain and support predictions and hypotheses, the student needs to be able to answer the question: "Why do you think this would happen?" To verify predictions or hypotheses, the student needs to be able to answer the questions: "What would it take for such a thing to be true? Would it be true in all cases? At what time?"

Prediction in reading is problem solving through conjecture and supposition via the knowledge given in text and from students' own background knowledge.

Strategy—What's Going to Happen?

Begin by collecting four or five objects that relate to an informational passage such as an article on the dangers of street racing. In this instance artifacts could include such items as a piece of twisted metal, a toy ambulance, a photo of skid marks and a picture of a sad person.

Share the objects with the students by bringing them out of a bag one at a time. Ask the students to describe each as it is passed around. Encourage a discussion based on the artifacts of predictions about the content of the informational passage. To supplement discussion, students can write out their guesses individually or, working in pairs, compare their predictions to others' in the group. Finally, read the passage then discuss it by verifying the successful predictions and refuting unsuccessful ones compared to the actual content.

The aim of this strategy is to strengthen the predicting ability of the students by enabling them to create a hypothesis about a topic based on clues gained from visual representations of aspects of the topic.

Strategy—A Word Makes a Difference

When a student miscues a word in a sentence, a passage can become unclear or illogical—all because of a lack of understanding one word. Using cloze strategy, help students predict missing words by beginning with a series of two-sentence selections with one important content word left out. For example:

- The boy brought his _____ to school to show his friends.
  During the lunch break they played a game of soccer.
- There were many _____ tracks in the snow.
  Some were from rabbits, some from mice; one was even a deer track.

Be sure to choose or create simple selections in which some of the words define another important content word within the selection. Challenge the students to focus on the clarifying words—the words that help us figure out the missing word. Emphasize how much power these words have to make meaning of the missing word. In the case above, "game" and "soccer" indicate "ball" and "rabbit," "mouse" and "deer" indicate "animal."

When students become proficient at this strategy, they may enjoy the challenge of creating longer more complicated passages to stump their classmates. The aim of the strategy is to learn to seek out words that clarify and help to make more reliable predictions about other text.

Data are collected not just to have heaps of information, but to provide opportunities to rethink and interpret, to hypothesize and predict what may yet come, and to observe the trends and patterns information may reveal.

Donald Graves,
educator and researcher

Focus on Research-Project Skills

The Missing Links

Once students have done their research on a topic, they need to be encouraged to look for gaps in their information. Using a jigsaw puzzle approach, have students think of the information they have found and then write items on small slips of paper as if these bits were pieces of a puzzle. Like in a jigsaw, a successful strategy is to put all the "like" pieces together, all the edges together, etc., thus making it easier to see what is there and what is missing.

Strategy—Fill the Gaps

The same approach can work for a research report. The only difference is that what is *not* there is what we must notice. Have students identify what information is actually stated in a report they have written, what they thought they had covered, and what others might like to know about the topic in order to decide if all that is needed is there. In other words, have they included enough information? After figuring out what might need to be added, another step would be to look for what is extraneous, what is repeated, and what could be deleted and not make any difference. All of these actions will make a cleaner, more cohesive research report.

Sometimes in school you may be asked to write about a subject that seems BORING. But give it a chance. Dig into it, do some research. When your curiosity is awakened, often a "boring" subject can become fascinating.
*Laurence Pringle, children's author
quoted in* Flora Wyatt

Teacher Realities

Info-Kids act out or hide out most often because of disinterest and boredom with what is going on in the classroom. We would be best advised to see these behaviors as an attempt to communicate that "what is going on here is not working for me." They cannot express their feelings in words, as knowing the school culture as they all do, they realize it is unacceptable to express lack of interest verbally. Become aware when the instruction content is engendering the acting out or fading out behavior and learn to avert these responses. Get them involved and connected to the instruction by piquing their interest through their interests.

Info-Kids Who Move to a Different Drummer

Einstein failed grade 2 too!

Characteristics

- Move to their own inner rhythm
- Evolve their own unique agenda and time schedule
- Live in their own world
- Develop a lifetime interest

Resources for Success

- Internet Web sites
- Encyclopedias and almanacs
- Idea books
- Comprehensive and in-depth resources
- Future prediction books
- "Cutting edge" books
- Reality-based science fiction and fantasy

Info-Kids who are the ultimate experts on a topic are unique and, without question, have their own inner rhythm, their own agenda and their own time schedule. Unusually confident in themselves, these students are very independent and inner-directed, to the point of being reclusive. Being so focused, it often seems as if they create a wall around themselves to pursue their interest without interference.

The topic is all—so much so that there is nothing else in their world. Being so immersed, they have no need to act out behaviorally. They do not cause trouble in the classroom other than their mind is seldom in attendance. There is every chance these kids will be the computer enthusiasts, the philosophical scientists and the theoretical mathematicians of the future.

Some of these Info-Kids are talkers, but more often they have little to say to others as they are so busy thinking. In either case, they may not like to read, particularly on topics outside their one specific area of interest, and often they do not like to write, even about their interest.

Meet the Info-Kids

Wanda—Under the Waves

Wanda is extremely mature for her age and has decided that she wants to become a marine biologist when she goes to university. In order to do this, according to her, she needs to know everything about whales, dolphins and life in the sea. She gets to spend her holidays at the family's beach cottage and has become fascinated by the marine life in the tidal pools.

Her compulsion has taken her through the books in the school library and the public library, and now she's in danger of being swamped on the Internet. She is realizing that there is so much information available that she must narrow her focus. Luckily, she is going to a biology camp for the summer as this will give her time to consider many areas. In the meantime, she has been watching nature programs on television, has become an avid user of the TV guides, and has taken up surfing the channels!

?

Ever been through a wormhole?

Then you're the first. "Wormhole" is the name given to the theory that the gravity of a very large object in space could curve space enough that it would turn back on itself, hence making travel in space from one point to another shorter.

Kyle—Caught in the Fourth Dimension!

Kyle is absorbed with "the dimensions." He compares and contrasts everything to the dimensions. During a class study on time, the teacher asked him to make a presentation to the class. He did so in such detail, using overheads and many resources, that the parents were invited to attend. He made a copy of the presentation as a booklet which is now being read and reread by others in the class. At the moment, he is absorbed in the 5th dimension, existing in a spatial grid of his own ….

Focus on Interests

Cutting Edge Information Is Tops

Info-Kids who move to a different drummer are fascinated with things on the cutting edge, particularly things that push the scientific edge, such as the paranormal, new discoveries in space, and the latest theories on dinosaurs. They become absorbed in exploring the Internet and pushing the edges of cyberspace. These kids often end up being our theorists—astrophysicists, paleontologists and philosophers.

Favorite Science Titles

- *Building Big* by David Macaulay
- *Eco-Fun: Great Projects, Experiments and Games for a Greener Earth* by David Suzuki and Kathy Vanderlinden
- *Electronics Lab: The Ultimate Electronics Pack* by Geoff Sida
- *Explorabook: A Kids Science Museum in a Book* by John Cassidy
- *Hidden Worlds: Looking through a Scientist's Microscope* by S. Kramer
- *Medicine* (Eyewitness) by Steve Parker
- *Nature Lab: The Ultimate Nature Pack*
- *Technology and Communications* (Datafiles) by Richard Platt
- *This Book Really Sucks!* by Jess Brallier

Strategy—Just Say NO!

A great entry point for success with Info-Kids who are fixated on one topic is for a teacher to pick up on a student's enthusiastic comment, "Did you know?" By hearing the eager tone of the comment and by simply stating a sincere "No," which requests clarification and more information, a teacher can encourage deeper exploration of the topic. Before you know it, the Info-Kid is off on a search for facts. Hence, through your active listening, an individual project, one he thinks he has chosen, begins.

Strategy—Montage of the Murky Deep

The oceans provide a source of so much interest to Info-Kids. Challenge students to create large ocean montages by cutting appropriate pictures from magazines.

These could be on any ocean-related themes, ranging from general views of the ocean to looking at natural wonders of the deep, barrier reefs, fish, or dangers to the ocean. Backgrounds could be designed from torn water-colored papers.

Focus on Resources

The Appeal of Adult References

Just because you are a kid shouldn't mean that a world of books is banned from you. The mere hint that adult titles may be too "hard" to read doesn't matter to these expert Info-Kids as they need access to books that go into a topic in depth.

Info-Kids who move to a different drummer have such a wealth of background knowledge that they have literally out-read their school library collections. In their obsession with a topic, they demand to have more specialized references to give them the new facts they require. They gravitate to selected adult titles, which they devour with greed and delight. Whoever said they had to read the whole book? These Info-Kids take from references what they want and pass over the rest.

This need for information also explains why the Internet has such appeal for these Info-Kids. They have a great sense of freedom, to go anywhere anytime, gleaning the facts they wanted to get or even those they did not know existed. Don't give me a simplified picture book when I want the real thing!

When I ask my students what they like about our class, they say "Book choice! You let us read what we want to read."

Sherry, teacher

Strategy—Don't Touch It! Don't Even Look at It!

Students often view adult books and resources as forbidden objects, probably because they have been repeatedly told to stay at their own reading level and not to look at them. Consequently, teachers are reluctant to use them in the classroom. Info-Kids covet these adult references as examples of the real world and want to be able to browse in them. These might include such items as *National Geographic* magazines, car magazines, humorous stories, or brochures about sports or travel, to name a few.

Invite your Info-Kids to bring their dad's favorite book or magazine to share. What does he like about it? What are his favorite parts? Better yet, why not invite him to come to share with the class? Moms are not excluded ... just extend the invitation!

Strategy—To the Edge ... and Beyond

For Info-Kids seeking information on space, time, parapsychology and other dimensions, look to some of the following:

Life on other planets, Giordano Bruno? We'll show you what we think of that idea! Who was Bruno and what happened to him?

Astronomer Giordano Bruno made public his idea in 1600. He was burned at the stake.

- Beecroft, Simon. *Super Humans: A Beginner's Guide to Bionics* (Future Files). A look at the technology behind robots and the possibility of mixing them with humans. Another title in the series is *Cosmic Journeys.*
- Bond, Peter. *DK Guide to Space.* "A photographic journey through the universe."
- Claybourne, Anna, et al. *The Usborne Book of the Paranormal.* A haunting glimpse of twenty cases featuring poltergeists, ESP, ghosts and aliens.
- Croswell, Ken. *See the Stars: Your First Guide to the Night Sky.* Follow the

Valentina Tereshkova, we look up to you. Who was she?

Valentina Tereshkova was the first woman in space.

If you leave Greeenwich, England traveling east, how many time zones will you cross before returning to Greenwich?

Twenty-four—there are 24 time zones on earth.

suggestions of a noted astronomer to find the secrets within the impressive photos of the constellations.

- Holland, Simon. *Space.* An up-to-the-minute view of what's out there, what we are moving through and what's coming at us.
- Johnstone, Michael. *The History News in Space.* Mock newspaper accounts of achievements in space, from the achievements of Ptolemy, Galileo and Von Braun, to recent plans for exploring Mars.
- Mitton, Jacqueline. *Aliens: The Facts behind the Fiction.* "Everything you've ever wanted to know about extraterrestrials—and some things you've never even dreamed of!"
- Nicolson, Cynthia Pratt. *Comets, Asteroids and Meteorites* (Starting With Space Series). Introduction to these cosmic phenomena with suggestions for activities and Internet sites.
- Royston, Angela. *Space Station: Accident on Mir* (DK Readers, Level 4). High drama as a breakdown threatens the existence of Mir. Photos and sidebars add to the informative content.
- Simon, Seymour. *Destination: Jupiter.* Current photos highlight this exploration of the planet and its moons.
- Swanson, Diane. *Nibbling on Einstein's Brain: The Good, the Bad & the Bogus in Science.* Leads to clear thinking about safe and unsafe products and services. Using science to detect the inadequate, the faulty and the phony.
- Trotman, Felicity. *Living in Space.* "A look into the International Space Station and other space stations past and present."

Strategy—Exploring the Oceans

Some titles which would intrigue an Info-Kid with a marine interest included the following:

- Day, Trevor. *Ocean* (Data Files). Facts, figures and information about this amazing world.
- Dewin, Ted. *Inside the Whale and Other Animals.* Impressive X-ray style drawings.
- Earle, Sylvia. *Dive! My Adventures in the Deep Frontier.* A view of the wonders of that last frontier—the ocean—with snorkel and dive gear, from the deep-sea laboratory *Tektite.*
- Ganeri, Anita. *The Oceans Atlas.* Explore the oceans above and below: effects of winds, waves, currents, tides, sea levels and shipping, as well as oil and gas exploration.
- Gray, Samantha. *Ocean* (Eye Wonder). From skimming the waves to the fissures in the deep—a look at the characteristics of our largest resource and its inhabitants.
- Markle, Sandra. *Pioneering Ocean Depths.* What do you find thousands of feet beneath the whitecaps?
- Maynard, Christopher. *Informania: Sharks.* Coil-bound, photo-filled compendium of shark facts.
- Pringle, Laurence. *Sharks! Strange and Wonderful.* There are more varieties than you can imagine.
- Sheikh-Miller, Jonathan. *Sharks* (Usborne Discovery). Follow hundreds of species, giants to minis, hunters to benign, as they swim through their environments.

- Simon, Seymour. *Sharks.* Large photos counteract print-dense text in this survey of the mammals.
- Stoops, Erik D. and Sherrie. *Sharks.* Rich photographic account of the shark's body, eating habits, senses, self-defense techniques, reproduction and relationship to humans.

Focus on Reading-Thinking Skills

Critical Reading

For some unknown reason we, adults and Info-Kids alike, believe anything in print is true and accurate. Yet, we also know it can be very inaccurate. Info-Kids need to be able to make judgments about the validity of a piece of writing. Critical reading is being able to evaluate the accurateness, currency or appropriateness of what is being read. Is the writing accurate and up-to-date, or misleading?

Students cannot do a good report if the information source is the 1985 *Guinness Book of Records*, and they need to know that. To judge the validity of information, students must select the facts that can enable them to compare the pros and cons, prioritize or rank the elements, decide, rate, criticize, argue, justify, assess and recommend. They will need to ask questions such as:

- Do you believe a person would ...?
- In your opinion ...?
- Could this ...?
- How might the author ...?

Strategy—I'm A Winner! Maybe?

We all get "junk mail" that makes outrageous claims or promises of the "you have just become a millionaire" or "pounds off forever" type. Read and discuss with students the claims and contents of one such advertisement. Ask questions such as:

- What do they mean by ...?
- Does ... sound true?
- Have you ever seen ...?

Recall the kinds of propaganda techniques that are used to sway people and explore them with your students. Some of these methods include: name calling through derogatory labels, vague glittering generalities, equating items with valued objects such as gold, testimonials with endorsements by famous people, bandwagon techniques, and card stacking on only one side of the story.

Bring in a lot of favorite magazines and flyers and you will see how easily students will able to locate techniques used in ads and junk mail. As students become more proficient at seeing false claims, they can look for more subtle examples of propaganda stratagies. Remember that not only words can lie—diagrams, charts and statistics can also be misleading and misconstrued.

The aim of this strategy is to encourage students to recognize propaganda techniques by evaluating the claims made in materials that enter their homes for accuracy.

There are so many things to discover in the world around you! Dr. Isaac Newton, the great scientist who discovered the laws of gravitation, once wrote: "I seem to be a boy playing on the seashore ... while the great ocean of truth lay all undiscovered before me." The ocean of truth is still waiting to be discovered.

Seymour Simon, children's author quoted in Flora Wyatt

Strategy—One Day Man Will Land on the Moon!

A provocative way to practise critical reading is to search the school library for samples of outdated information. The challenge is to secretly find pieces of mis-information, which are often found in the oldest reference books about specific topics. Have the students search to find sources from previous decades on such topics as landing on the moon or the names of countries in Eastern Europe, and to identify any misinformation. In most libraries, misconceptions about history, geography and science abound.

The aim of this strategy is to increase the students' awareness as to how many of the sources we depend on for information are not current and are incorrect.

Focus on Research-Project Skills

What Are the Real Facts?

Once all the facts within a research project are there and covered, it is time to see if each one is fact or opinion, truth or belief. Facts found on Web sites are especially suspect as sites come and go quickly, and, unless their source is pres-tigious and reliable, it is mostly a matter of just believing in their validity. The obvious path to check the facts in a research project is to compare one source against one or more other sources. Some excellent discussions and in-depth searches can be started this way.

Strategy—Don't Believe Everything You Read

Comparing sources can lead students to the realization that not all that is written is fact and truth. What is written and the way it is slanted depends on the author's intent. An interesting exercise is to present students with a fact (e.g., the number of elephants being poached in Africa is on the increase), have them research the topic and write a paragraph on it, and then challenge them to turn the paragraph into a persuasive advertisement. For example, the elephants dilemma mentioned above could be slanted to bilk money from the unsuspect-ing. By creating nonsense, students will be better able to recognize it in the "real" world.

What worked: individualizing—giving choice and control when creating the assignment, acknowledging interest area. What didn't: he remained separate from the class (partly due to his introverted nature). He continued to have his own interests and wanted to function separately from the group. He didn't like to read fiction books, although he enjoyed our read-alouds. His mother read stories to him at home to support his novel studies.

Cathie, teacher

Teacher Realities

Some Info-Kids are so immersed in their particular interest that they won't focus on anything else. Our best response is to go with it. Listen to their enthusiasm and tie instruction to it. Be as flexible as possible about time limits and deadlines. Often the concept of organizing time has no meaning to these students.

Use anything that can keep their focus on the project at hand. The actual physical use of a computer can sometimes help. Yet accept when they must go their own way in their own time. More actual learning will be accomplished when you can be this flexible. Einstein did, after all, survive failing grade two.

CHAPTER 11

Info-Kids Who Gravitate to the Gross

Cool! That's SO gross!

Characteristics
- Seek out the unusual and bizarre
- Push edges of acceptability
- Challenge cultural beliefs
- Delight in the rude and the taboo
- Cover up their interests and reactions through humor

Resources for Success
- Gross books
- Slightly rude books
- Bathroom books
- "Bawdy" body books
- Disaster titles
- Bizarre trivia

Some Info-Kids delight in things on the thin edge of the wedge. These students are absorbed by the unusual and fascinated by the forbidden—the weird, the taboo and the gross! We might say they seem off the wall in this regard, but perhaps their interest is more an intrigue with the unknown, the unspeakable and the forbidden of adult topics.

One thing certain is that they react and cover up through humor. Each example they find of weird facts or wacky information will be followed by hoots of laughter, raucous revelry and gusts of giggles that seem to suggest: "Listen to me. I know what adults know too, and I am brave enough to speak of the unspeakable!" They are pushing the edges of their knowledge as they push the edges of acceptability.

Fascination with disasters is a similar edge, but of a different kind. The things that happen in disasters are unspeakable, but intriguing as well. To understand this, just think of how many adults listen to the "disastrous" news programs each night. Perhaps this is just a more grown-up version of monsters under the bed—a way to keep awake and interested in a routine life.

Meet the Info-Kids

Jason—This Book Sucks!

Jason uses this word over and over. To him everything s....! Everything at home, in his life, at school, at the mall—it all s....! One day his teacher told him she had a book for him that he would hate because it really s...ed! He didn't stand a chance. He was hooked right away. So what if the idea behind the book is an exploration of the topic of suckers: people who are easily fooled, something that pulls with force upon something else, and a North American freshwater fish? *This Book Really Sucks!* features "the science behind gravity, flight, leeches, black holes, tornadoes, our friend the vacuum cleaner, and just about everything else that sucks"—all within a rubber, suction-cup-covered cover.

Jason got so involved in this book that he decided to create his own book on gas ... or to be specific, the expansion qualities of gas. Be careful ... this book will probably have a tendency to fart! The humor of double meanings, colloquial expressions and word play is not lost on this student, nor his classmates.

Rob—It Was So Big and ... It's Gone!

Rob is the kind of kid who likes large objects—ships, airplanes and buildings. The appeal is that they give a sense of permanence and, even though machines run them, they are not machine-like.

What absorbs his interest, however, are the disasters where huge objects are destroyed. For awhile the Titanic was his main interest. He devoured every morsel of information he could glean from books, the Internet, newspaper accounts, old photographs and, of course, the feature-length movie. He was consumed by the structure of the ship and its navigational devices, and he frequently speculated as to what it would have been like to be on it. Other great ship disasters, including the one described in the movie *The Poseidon Adventure,* were tops on his list.

Recently, along with the rest of the world, he has been emotionally overwhelmed by the tragic events of the World Trade Center in New York. The repeated images of the scene haunt him, as well as his teachers. How could this happen? Now he is caught up in the structural considerations of the major skyscrapers around the world. How could the terrorists know that steel would melt at 1,500 degrees Fahrenheit and precisely where to hit the buildings for maximum effect?

Focus on Interests

The Dirt on Gross Facts

Info-Kids relish taboo topics and adult facts they aren't supposed to know. They seek out prohibited words and information, trying for one-upmanship over their friends. They hide their use of inappropriate language and accompanying behavior with laughter. Everything on the taboo side produces snickers and giggles. Along with this often comes a fascination with disasters, both human and natural. These Info-Kids delight in knowing every facet of devastating events. The challenge is to find ways to capitalize on seemingly unorthodox interests to promote learning and literacy.

> **When I was a kid making silly books out in the hall, I never dreamed that one day I'd be making silly books for a living. The coolest thing is that I used to get in trouble for being the class clown … and now it's my job.**
>
> *Dav Pilkey, children's author writing on his Web site—www.pilkey.com*

Favorite Gross Books

- *The Book of Slime* by Ellen Jackson
- *Dirt and Grime* by Vicki Cobb
- *Grossology: The Science of Really Gross Things!* by Sylvia Branzei
- *The Really Hairy Scary Spider and Other Creatures with Lots of Legs* by Theresa Greenaway
- *Skin That Slimes and Scares* (Up Close) by Diane Swanson
- *Why Is Soap So Slippery? And Other Bathtime Questions* by Catherine Ripley
- *That Really Fearsome Blood-loving Vampire Bat and Other Creatures with Strange Eating Habits* by Theresa Greenaway
- *The Truly Tasteless Scratch and Sniff Book*

Strategy—You Louse

The language of kids on the playground could curl your hair! Swearing is in, especially the "F" and "S" words. When we think about it, the continuous repetition of certain words is merely a lack of ability to use the English language creatively. Challenge students to create an Insulter's Glossary or Offender's Dictionary of non-swear words that really do offend others. Suggest that the students practise using diminutives (e.g., you little, tiny, squirt, etc.) to get them started.

It's all about how to swear without swearing!

Strategy—It's A Disaster!

Don't ask why, but some Info-Kids have a fascination with disasters. They want to know all the gory details, and have a vivid memory for them much later. One successful approach for capturing the attention of such students is to read aloud a description of a major disaster, and to see if at the end of it they can identify what it is. Yes, they can shout it out, but why not encourage them to write their answer on a piece of paper, thus getting them connecting to writing? One has to be careful about revealing certain information—merely mentioning April 14, 1912 … and the name Titanic will burst forth!

Focus on Resources

Choice, Junk and Censorship

What difference does it make, if the book is good or not, as long as they are reading?

Mary, teacher

If it works—use it! We as teachers are often so attuned to placing emphasis on quality books, we forget that we view books through adult lenses. Info-Kids have a very different viewpoint, often finding interest and value in "in-our-eyes" trashy materials. If truth were known, we might be quite shocked at the poor quality of writing and stereotypical, cartoon-style illustrations found in items they pick up. But, we must remember that our objective is to improve the reading ability of these Info-Kids. Let's turn the other cheek (or eye!), accept their selections, and get them discussing the content of the books. We should, of course, read their choices so that we know what is in the books and, also, to gain respect from them that we will read their preferences.

Accepting what students read has its moments! After all, many Info-Kids do gravitate to fairly gross materials—perhaps including some off-color, rude, tasteless items. This brings up the threat of censorship, which despite having the most educated general public in our history, is increasing from both the right and the left. Many individuals seem to think they have the right to decide what somebody's else's children cannot read. As a teacher, don't panic. There should be a selection policy in place in each school and district which provides for parental challenges. Ask your principal to show it to you. We have found in our experience that it is usually only the materials which are read aloud to the entire class or which are required to be read by the whole class that cause problems.

As professionals, we need to know what resources are being used in the classroom and to decide if they are appropriate for the age group and the community. At the same time, without stomping on individuals who like junk or popular literature, we have seen intermediate teachers getting students excited about resources and issues that would intrigue adults too. It's all up to you!

Everybody loves a good laugh—bawdy books provide for it, as they give us a fresh look at life around us. If you have a Jason or two in your class, try:

- Bailey, Linda. *Adventures with the Vikings* (Good Times Travel Agency). Humorous happenings as the Binkerton kids arrive back in Viking days.
- Deary, Terry. *Horrible Histories: The Vicious Vikings*. Hilarious account of their invasion of the savage Saxon lands.
- Hickman, Pamela. *Animals Eating: How Animals Chomp, Chew, Slurp and Swallow*. Feeling hungry? Consider this.
- Katz, Alan. *Take Me Out of the Bathtub and Other Silly Dilly Songs*. Poems that will make you yuck or laugh—"The Yoghurt Flies Straight from My Brother," "Ripped My Favorite T-Shirt" and "Sock in the Gravy."
- Lauber, Patricia. *What You Never Knew about Tubs, Toilets and Showers*. A dirty history of what happened after the fall of Rome when the filthy decline set in! Hilarious.
- Scott, Tim. *History Hoaxes*. A warning on the cover says it all—the book contains ridiculous fakes and total lies.
- Solheim, James. *It's Disgusting and We Ate It! True Food Facts from around the World—and throughout History!* Soups such as earthworm and bird's-nest, followed by flower salad with fungus, are just the beginning of the delights. Mind you, some are just rotten!
- Swanson, Diane. *Animals Eat the Weirdest Things*. Don't look at this one over a meal.

Strategy—Bawdy Body Books

And then there are books about the human body—another almost rude, almost taboo edge to explore. Consider some of these:

- Baggaley, Ann, ed. *Human Body*. 700 photos tell it like it is (or 700 photos show us what we are!).
- *Body: Bones, Muscle, Blood and Other Body Bits* (Secret Worlds). How does our body work?
- Funston, Sylvia. *The Book of You. The Science of Why You Look, Feel and Act the Way You Do*. How do you and your body measure up?
- Jennings, Gael. *Bloody Moments: Highlights from the Astonishing History of Medicine*. A humorous, tongue-in-cheek, choose-your-own-adventure look at the history of medicine and medical discoveries, from the first bloodletting to designer transplants.
- Nicolson, Cynthia Pratt. *Mysterious You Baa! The Most Interesting Book You'll Ever Read about Genes and Cloning*. DNA, cells and us.
- Parker, Steve. *The Body Atlas*. Large, well-labeled, detailed illustrations of all parts of our body.
- Platt, Richard. *Stephen Biesty's Incredible Body: Meet the Teams That Make the Body Work!* Two tiny explorers go inside the body and find six teams at work (blood, immune, nerve, hormone, etc.) Incredible detail.
- Swanson, Diane. *Burp? The Most Interesting Book You'll Ever Read about Eating*. It's all a matter of "in" and "out" (Yuck!).
- Swanson, Diane. *Hmm? The Most Interesting Book You'll Ever Read about Memory*. Don't forget—read this book!

It is said the sky was covered with these birds, but they were completely wiped out by American hunters by 1914. What bird was it and what happened to it?

The passenger pigeon used to be a delicacy. Now it is extinct forever due to overhunting and urbanization.

Can you live with a hole in your stomach?

Alexis St. Martin lived for over 40 years with a hole in his stomach. A doctor put food on a silk string into the wound to see how the stomach acted on food.

- Walker, Richard. *The Children's Atlas of the Human Body: Actual Size Bones, Muscles and Organs in Full Color.* Fold out chart is the highlight.
- Walker, Richard. *DK Guide to the Human Body: A Photographic Journey through the Human Body.* The lungs, joints, blood … are put into a new perspective.
- Walker, Richard. *3-D Human Body.* The use of a mirror set in the middle of two images makes body parts appear as three-dimensional objects.

Strategy—Meet My Mummy

We are all fascinated with bodies, and those that have lasted for a long time receive even more attention. How exciting it must have been to have uncovered a mummy, wondering all the time who he or she was and why they had received such special treatment on death. Here are some titles about mummies to get your students started:

- Bailey, Linda. *Adventures in Ancient Egypt.* Opening a book in a strange travel agency is the key for three youngsters to be transported back to the banks of the Nile for further adventures.
- Berger, Melvin and Guilda. *Mummies of the Pharaohs: Exploring the Valley of the Kings.* Famous tombs are uncovered, revealing fabulous treasures besides their occupants.
- Macdonald, Fiona. *Mummies and Tombs* (Discovery). Egyptian mummies and their relatives in other parts of the world: a glimpse at death beliefs, coffins, tombs and mummified bodies of humans and animals. Step-by-step craft projects.
- *Mummies and the Secrets of Ancient Egypt* (Secret Worlds). How to prepare your mum!
- Steele, Philip. *The Best Book of Mummies.* At last—how to preserve a body so that it becomes a mummy.
- Tanaka, Shelley. *Secrets of the Mummies: Uncovering the Bodies of Ancient Egyptians.* Follow the mummy hunters as they search for treasures and unwrap their finds. Who were those that were given this honor?

Strategy—What Blew Up?

Need some help to become conversant about disasters? Check out the following disastrous books!

- Bonson, Richard, and Richard Platt. *Disaster! Catastrophes That Shook the World.* The worst disasters that were weather- or human-related. Includes some famous ones in history.
- Levithan, David. *In the Heart of the Quake* (Disaster Zone Books). Are you ready for a good shake up?
- Newson, Lesley. *The Atlas of the Worlds' Worst Natural Disasters.* Extensive coverage of the effects of the shifting earth, violent skies and weather-related chaos.
- Nicolson, Cynthia Pratt. *Volcano!* Hot eruption spots—some old, some happening today.
- Piven, Joshua, and David Borgenicht. *The Worst-Case Scenario Survival Handbook.* The place to go when confronted with the dilemmas of how to

If you were Tutankhamen, how many coffins would it take to encase your mummy?

Three.

After our earthquake they couldn't stop reading about it—even on the Web.

April, teacher

?

This eruption made its victims volcanic prisoners for 1700 years. What was it?

Vesuvius, in 79 A.D.

fend off a shark, jump from a moving car, escape from killer bees, and many other survival situations.

- Simon, Seymour. *Tornadoes.* The causes and results of the family of twisters, dust devils, whirlwinds, waterspouts and cyclones.
- Tanaka, Shelley. *The Buried City of Pompeii: What It Was Like When Vesuvius Exploded.* Where were they when the eruption happened?
- Tanaka, Shelley. *On Board the Titanic.* Photo insights into the structure of the ship and where the people were at the time of the collision.
- *Tornadoes and Other Dramatic Weather Systems* (Secret Worlds). Wild weather warnings.

Focus on Reading-Thinking Skills

Inferring

Inferring is figuring out what has been left out and what the author does not tell us, but we should be able to guess from the clues given in the text. It is about finding the gaps and realizing what should be in them. When inferring, we use our background knowledge together with clues the author has given to infer missing but logical information. Basically, inference is reading between the lines and answering the "why" questions.

Strategy—Invisible Messages

What do we mean by invisible messages? Invisible messages are what the author has left out yet expects the reader to figure out from what is in the text and their own background knowledge. These are rather like the clues that pop up in a mystery story.

Starting from a passage like the one on lightning below, have students read the paragraph and brainstorm information that is left out but that they can deduce from reading the paragraph and drawing on their own knowledge.

> "Say 'lightning strike' aloud. That takes about a second. Every second of every day, lightning strikes Earth an average of one hundred times. Most storms break out in warm and wet areas." (from Hopping, Lorrain Jean. *Lightning!*)

In pairs, groups, or on their own, have students write down as many inferences as they can make from the passage as possible. For example:

- Lightning strikes the Earth about 80,000 times per day
- We have fewer storms than Florida because we have a cooler and drier climate

List their inferences on the board. Challenge students to defend or refute the appropriateness of each inference by supporting their inferences with context clues and background knowledge.

The aim of this strategy is to enhance students' abilities to infer implied information when reading and to help them become aware of the many possible inferences that can be made in even a short passage.

Strategy—I Thought You Thought!

An interesting aspect of inference is interpretation. Cartoon strips, political cartoons and some picture books depend on the illustrations to give a different meaning from the words. Collect cartoon strip models and have students interpret the differences between the words and the illustrations. Be prepared for much laughter and groans! Encourage pairs of students to try the process themselves.

A next step is to share cartoons without captions and challenge students to write their own. These could be compared to the originals to see if any inferences were lost. To make the task a little more complex, have students create thought bubbles for each of the characters in the strip.

The point of this strategy is to help students learn how to interpret the inferences that lie between illustrations and text.

Focus on Research-Project Skills

Size Matters

Research projects fall into two types—those that are too short and those that are too long. Students often tend to either not put enough detail into their work or to add so much detail that the important points are camouflaged completely. Both these tendencies, once recognized, can be remedied. One way is through becoming aware of audience. Who will be the reader? Peers? Teacher? Parents? Younger children? The type of audience intended will help determine how a project is written and presented.

Strategy—Will the Real Audience Please Stand Up?

No matter who the audience is, students need to pay attention to the vocabulary used and to its appropriateness for the individuals in the group. Otherwise their message and main points may be lost or overlooked by those unable to get past the words used. For example:

- Is it too complex or too simple?
- Is it specific enough or too general?
- Should scientific names, common names or both be used?
- Has jargon been avoided?
- Is there slang that needs to be eliminated?
- Are dynamic, rather than boring, verbs, adjectives and adverbs used?
- Are words used appropriately?
- Do words mean what you mean for them to mean?
- Are complex ideas defined within the text?

One good way to find out if the vocabulary and the audience have been correctly matched throughout a written project is to have students try it out on one person who represents their selected audience. If that person does not understand, likely the rest of the students' audience at that level won't either.

Stephen King is attractive precisely because he is risky. ... the gesture of limit testing is a time-honored tradition among at-risk students.

John Skretta, educator

Teacher Realities

Teachers are the arbitrators of what is "correct" only in that we reflect the culture we teach in. What are considered acceptable behaviors, language or topics to study change continually. We may very well be behind the times.

We need to develop more open and less censorious minds to be able to work successfully with Info-Kids, as they often like to investigate the quirky and are drawn to the taboo. Learn to back off and resist making value judgments. Why forbid a book like Sylvia Branzei's *Grossology?* Who cares? Reading it is not a life or death issue. This type of interest, too, will pass.

Info-Kids Who Picture the World

Hey, look at that!

Characteristics

- Require visual rather than aural approaches to learning
- Love to doodle
- Watch television endlessly
- Enjoy playing video games
- Are intrigued by design, pattern and color

Resources for Success

- Picture books for older readers
- Visual dictionaries
- Wordless picture books
- Videos
- Photo essays
- Graphic novels and comics

We live in a visually-focused world, so it is no wonder that many students are primarily visual learners, surrounded as they are by a multitude of visual images—ads, television, videos .... Without a doubt, some Info-Kids learn by what they see—they would rather watch than hear. Those who have been reared by video nannies and television babysitters rapidly turn into passive viewing addicts. The result? Couch potatoes by age 13!

The good news is that these visual Info-Kids are easily and readily caught up in the many highly visual information books that are currently available. One just has to have a cross-section book on a table and students will become absorbed in looking at the detailed cut-away illustrations. There is also an entire genre of picture books evolving for older readers (and adults), which offers Info-Kids a visual challenge and, through the illustrations, an entry into written text.

Meet the Info-Kids

Dale—Media Man

Dale is a quiet grade seven student who just exists in school, remaining almost invisible to his teachers. But underneath his comatose exterior, he is a particularly visually astute youngster. He regularly assists the teacher-librarian on a media team.

Dale is a visual learner. Fortunately for him, the teacher-librarian has encouraged him to explore the video resources available from the district resource centre. Dale is allowed to order whatever he wants to view. As a result, munching on lunch in a "private viewing den," he and other media team members are able to view hundreds of videos. Gradually, the teacher-librarian has encouraged his teachers to use Dale's expertise to order materials for their curriculum units. He has also been involved in critiquing preview copies of new videos for the school district. Although his English teacher originally thought his writing performance showed a lack of ability, she changed her mind when she allowed Dale to share his video experiences as part of class assignments.

I believe that by being provided with the freedom to plan and pursue their direction of study, and being respected and reinforced within the classroom community for their efforts, Carl and Angus were empowered and their self efficacy increased immensely.

Debra, teacher

Carl and Angus—Knights of the Night

Carl and Angus are capable readers, but generally lack the drive that results in excellent performance. Though they read novels, their lack of enthusiasm for discussions, independent reading programs, written responses, etc., is noticeable.

One day, however, they expressed an interest in reading nonfiction materials about castles, knights and medieval times. They ended up doing in-depth research on their own, using the school library resources, the public library and the Internet for information. They spent hours during class time and out of school reading about and discussing designs, history, weaponry, architecture and other aspects of medieval life. Their parents reported that they often worked late into the night to complete some of the aspects of the project.

After about a month and a half of research and work, the boys had created a wonderful project entitled "Castle" that included an excellent poster, illustrations and well-organized information. They also created weapons on a real-life scale. Carl and Angus presented their information with enthusiasm and fielded questions from the class adeptly, answering with expansive explanations that they were able to support with text and pictorial references.

Focus on Interests

Surfing Interests

Info-Kids who are highly visually-oriented—both because of being visual learners and because of the impact of media on their lives—appear to surf a broad range of interests. Just as with television, one click is all it takes and a new topic pops up for a quick look or a long stare. Many of these kids are interested in the visualization of history as it puts our world into perspective and allows us to see people and events from a different viewpoint. Medieval times is a popular historical topic. Art, too, gives us a sensory interpretation in a different medium.

Strategy—I Get My Narrative Nonfiction on Video

Many students, particularly older intermediate students, start to go through a cocoon stage of life where they want to "veg out" in front of the television. Videos are big in their lives. Even on a sunny day, there they are in the twilight zone watching videos. Many have quite expansive tastes—just as long as they are watching. Although they will not pick up a novel to read voluntarily, they will watch the video of it.

Students can be challenged to film a short documentary feature on a natural happening in their community. For instance, beavers cutting down trees in a favorite park or an outbreak of coyotes in the city might intrigue. However, stay away from the skunks! Insights into the process of making a video can be found in references such as Robin Cross's *Movie Magic* and Lisa O'Brien's *Lights, Camera, Action!*

Of prime importance is a quality camera person. A useful source for improving picture taking is Neil Johnson's *Photography Guide for Kids*. When creating a video with students, start with the basics and encourage them to consult information books for background—gleaning lists of terminology, suggestions for camera shots and ideas for action scenes to more clearly present the content.

?

So, why a kinetoscope, Mr. Edison?

Thomas Edison invented the kinetoscope, a peephole film viewer, which he thought would make more money since people could watch the film only one at a time.

Introducing a wordless book to struggling readers is sometimes a shock to their understanding of what reading is. When these students come to realize that they can "read" a book, even though it has no words of its own, they begin to realize what reading is—and that they can do it!

Judith Cassady, educator

Strategy—Errors in the Past?

So, you think you know your history, eh? A remarkable resource for visual information is *Errata: A Book of Historical Errors,* written by S.A.J. Wood and illustrated by Hemesh Alles. Portrayed are a dozen time periods, ranging from farming on the Nile, to the return of an Inca army, a Viking funeral, a 1066 Norman feast, a Zulu wedding, an emperor's visit to the Great Wall of China, to a Sioux encampment on the Great Plains—but all with a difference.

Hemesh Alles's illustrations are filled with a myriad details, but if you look carefully, you'll note that there are some things that are not quite right! For example, at a Norman feast on Christmas Day in 1066, you would not have found a Christmas tree, a television set, playing cards, or even spoons. At the Zulu wedding, you would not have found a man wearing a belt or a metal shield, or a Zulu woman wearing a heart-shaped gold locket as jewelry. Students will accept the challenge readily to search out those things that are just too modern for the times. Comparisons with information books about the time periods will enhance the search. And for the teachers? Well, they have a secret source of information—it is called the answer key at the back of the book!

Once Info-Kids get the basic idea for this approach, they can undertake to design error-filled historical scenes of their own—trying to stump their fellow students, and even their parents.

Strategy—There's More Than You Can See!

Info-Kids need to have their attention focused on how an illustrator can go beyond the text. Ask questions such as:

• Does the illustrator tell the same story as the author?
• Is the mood appropriate?
• Are the characters responsive to the action?
• Are feelings and emotions effectively conveyed?
• Are multiple levels of meaning evident?

Info-Kids need to learn to read the illustrations as well as the text. Why not suggest they look at the illustrations only as they flip through the book, trying to detect the story line, the mood, the theme and the changing flow of the focus?

What better way to make students aware of the styles and artistic merits of illustrations than to look at (study!) the work of one illustrator or illustrative team. The remarkable artistic team of Bonnie and Arthur Geisert has created an exciting quartet of books about towns—*Prairie Town, River Town, Mountain Town* and *Desert Town*—which would work well for such a study. The intriguing illustrations are hand-colored, copper-plate etchings that show the changes in each town over the period of one year.

These pictures are not static. We guarantee that you will not even be remotely close to observing the number of happenings and changes occurring over the pages. Dozens of vignettes and stories within stories are interspersed throughout each book depicting details of ordinary life. You and your students will have to look again and again to see them. How exciting it is when someone finds something new—everyone has to look again. Thankfully, the illustrators have given us some clues in their comments at the end of the book.

Encourage students to find other picture books that are filled with small details. They will remember the *Where's Waldo* books from their younger days.

Favorite Dragon/Beast Titles
- *The Discovery of Dragons* by Graeme Base
- *Dragons Are Singing Tonight* by Jack Prelutsky
- *Fabulous Monsters* by Marcia Williams
- *Fantastic Beasts and Where to Find Them* by Newt Scamander

Favorite Art Books
- *The Art Gallery of Ontario. Meet the Group of Seven* by David Wistow and Kelly McKinley
- *The Art of Science: A Pop-Up Adventure in Art* by Jay Young
- *The History of Making Books* (Voyages of Discovery)
- *How Are You Peeling? Foods with Moods* by Saxton Freymann and Joost Elffers
- *The Impressionists: The Origins of Modern Painting* (Masters of Art) by Francesco Salvi
- *National Gallery of Art Activity Book: 25 Adventures with Art* by Maura A. Clarkin
- *Now You See It, Now You Don't: The Amazing World of Optical Illusions* (rev. ed.) by Seymour Simon
- *Renaissance* (Eyewitness Books) by Andrew Langley

Strategy—St. George to the Rescue

Famous artists have delighted in the challenge of portraying medieval times and one of its heroes, St. George. Thus, Dutch painter Rogier van der Weyden (1399-1464) created a tiny treasure of "St. George and the Dragon" (1432-35). This painting, rich in detail, shows a damsel in distress watching as armor-clad St. George drives his spear through the neck of a small dragon on a hillside overlooking a walled town by a lake shore.

There is so much to see in this painting. Challenge students to discover a skull, the dragon's teeth, Saint George's spurs, two people on horseback and two ships. What else might they find in the painting? You could use an "I Spy" technique—giving a clue and daring others to find an item in question, as well as other details. Consult Maura Clarkin's *National Gallery of Art Activity Book* or some of the other art books listed for more ideas with great paintings, or the books suggested for depictions of dragons and other beasts.

Focus on Resources

Picture Books for Older Readers

Don't make the mistake of thinking that picture books are only for little kids! Far from it! Teachers need to realize that if they start appreciating and reading picture books aloud to older students, the "baby" labels will come off and students will feel relaxed to enjoy the delights they have to offer.

The leading artists in the world are designing picture books for older readers, aiming at the "kid" in all of us. Much of the humor in picture books is adult humor with its wit and sophistication. These artists design picture books because they love creating a work of art that appeals to all ages. Many want the challenge of integrating the format and the text together, as well as the challenge of integrating the nonfiction information the stories are based on into the illustrations. They quickly realize that they will receive far more response from this art form than from any of their "fine art" creations.

Strategy—Picture Books to Inspire

Fortunately for all of us, there are magnificently-rendered nonfiction and fiction picture books based on fact that are constantly being published that have great appeal. These splendiferous visualizations are stunning to look at, beautiful to behold and evoke a sense of wonder and aesthetic appreciation for beauty. Encourage students to share what they like about these beautiful books, to take them home to share with their families, and to return with comments from their parents and grandparents. Here are a few worth sharing:

- Base, Graham. *Animalia.* A classic favorite of youngsters. Each page featuring a letter of the alphabet is filled with a visual chaos of objects and beasts.
- Dillon, Leo and Diane. *To Every Thing There Is a Season: Verses from Ecclesiastes.* Authors share distinctive cultural images.
- Jenkins, Steve. *Slap, Squeak and Scatter: How Animals Communicate.* Although done in a simplistic style, dramatic cut and torn paper images heighten the communication process.

Favorite Visual Dictionaries

• *Dictionary of the Earth* by John Farndon
• *Dictionary of Nature* by David Barnie
• *The Dorling Kindersley Children's Illustrated Dictionary*
• *The Junior Visual Dictionary* by Jean-Claude Corbeil
• *Star Wars: The Visual Dictionary* by David West Reynolds
• *The Stoddart Visual Dictionary* by Jean-Claude Corbeil
• *The Visual Dictionary of Cars* (Eyewitness Visual Dictionaries)

?

The Japanese air attack on Pearl Harbor knocked out 7 ships and over 100 airplanes. How long did this feat take?

It took just under two hours!

• Sturges, Philemon. *Bridges Are to Cross.* This book has fifteen dramatic paper-cut bridges guaranteed to intrigue and inspire.
• Wick, Walter. *A Drop of Water: A Book of Science and Wonder.* "The most spectacular photographs ever created on the subject of water."
• Whatley, Bruce and Rosie Smith. *Whatley's Quest.* Delight in this book as an apple (A) gets shot across the pages of this lavish alphabetical exploration.

And finally, Paul O. Zelinsky's *Rapunzel* is reminiscent of French and Italian masterpieces—rich, evocative paintings capture the plight of the maiden waiting in her tower.

Strategy—Visualize the Past

A recent trend is an increase in picture books that portray a moment in time, be it the depression, a war, or Ancient Egypt. Why in a picture book? Don't be easily fooled. Picture book writers and illustrators take a great deal of time and effort to place a major event, era or culture within its accurate time period, highlighting the essential information needed to gain an understanding of what took place.

The illustrations, if they are outstanding, will be filled with specific details, such as those allowing students to recognize objects their grandparents may have used and stored away. Ask questions such as:

• What objects or settings can be readily identified?
• Which objects or settings might the teacher recognize?
• How can you prove that the illustrators did their research?
• Are the illustrations accurate in their details?

Challenge Info-Kids to check out museums, galleries or the Internet, or to consult adult references to verify the visual facts. The aim of this strategy is to have Info-Kids glean as much accurate information from the background illustrations as they can. The illustrations then become a means of personalizing history, making it more relevant to readers.

Go with the past! What can you tell about the times in these picture books based on facts?

• Bunting, Eve. *So Far from the Sea.* A remarkable reflection of a Japanese American family driving to Utah to show the children where the parents were interned during the Second World War. Chris Soentpiet's illustrations reflect both the colorful present and the black-and-white reality of the 1940s after the attack on Pearl Harbor.
• Kroeger, Mary Kay, and Louise Borden. *Paperboy.* Set in Cincinnati, at the time of the big fight between ex-champ Jack Dempsey and "Gentleman Gene" Tunney, young Willie tries to help his family with money earned from being a paperboy. Ted Lewin's illustrations are full of the times—clothing, street cars, Model 'A' Fords and appropriate kitchen appliances.
• Wheatley, Nadia. *My Place.* An award-winning account of a young girl in a small Australian town. Each change of page shows the house and community another decade back in time. This time venture stops two hundred years earlier with the Aboriginal peoples in possession of the land.

You're the last person to get into the full house at Circus Maximus to see the Roman gladiators battle to death. What number are you?

Believe it or not, number 250,000!

- Wilkes, Angela. *A Farm through Time: The History of a Farm from Medieval Time to the Present Day.* Unfold history and find out how farming has changed the landscape, and how farming itself has changed yet, in some ways, stayed the same.

Strategy—Make Mine Medieval

Have you ever wondered what it was really like to live in the Middle Ages? Would we have liked to live then? What were the good times? What were the awful aspects of life? How were kids treated?

Info-Kids want to know the answers to these questions, but it is often difficult to get an accurate sense of them from strictly fact-focused accounts. We can make it easier for students by turning to a trio of novels by Karen Cushman. Professionally a medievalist by training, Cushman's novels have an accuracy of fact, a dependability for reality and an inherent sense of the world as seen through the eyes of her characters.

As they, or you, read *Matilda Bone, Catherine Called Birdy* or *The Midwife's Apprentice,* encourage students to mentally note the facts about daily life, including food, clothing, houses, activities, etc. Later, lead them back into the books to verify and discuss the realities of the times. Novels such as these can be used to complete the basic impressions presented by fact books.

It is important to relate the facts in novels to the actual realities occurring at the time. For example, architecture was a major aspect of medieval daily life, what with the crucial significance of castles for protection and security, and of massive cathedrals intended to bring glory to the Almighty. David Macaulay's splendid books *Castle* and *Cathedral: The Story of Its Construction* give much insight into these lasting memorials. Also, his *Building the Book Cathedral* provides many sketches and original designs for the book.

To explore the medieval period, play the ballad "Greensleeves" in the background and invite your students to peruse the following titles:

- Bergin, Mark. *Castle* (Fast Forward). The role and life of knights is revealed with flip pages heightening the action.
- Byam, Michele. *Arms and Armor* (Eyewitness Books). Crossbows, axes, daggers, swords, and plate and mail armor from the early Dark Ages to the end of the Middle Ages—and after.
- Langley, Andrew. *Castle at War: the Story of a Siege.* Make haste, the enemy comes! Highly detailed illustrations view the successful resistance of an attack and siege.
- Osborne, Will, and Mary Pope. *Knights and Castles: A Nonfiction Companion to the Knight at Dawn* (Magic Tree House Research Guide #2). A clever introduction to life in the Middle Ages designed for readers of the novel.
- Platt, Richard (transcriber). *Castle Diary: The Journal of Tobias Burgess, Page.* In 1285, a young lad enters his uncle's castle to learn the many skills needed to become a squire or even a knight. His education succeeds—with a few jolts—as witnessed in the droll caricature illustrations.
- Platt, Richard. *Stephen Biesty's Cross-Sections: Castle.* The challenge in each illustration is to find the spy.
- Steele, Philip. *Castles.* Castles, their towns, and the people defending and living within them. Lively sections on building, markets, becoming a knight, heraldry, siege strategy and many facets of life.

It's hard to get good help! How many people were on the indoor staff of Windsor Castle during the 1400s?

Over 400!

Would a knight ever let himself be seen with a destrier?

Absolutely! A destrier was a powerful horse used by knights as a warhorse.

- Tanaka, Shelley. *In the Time of Knights.* The life and times of one of the greatest English knights, William Marshal.
- Williams, Brian. *Forts and Castles.* A survey of world forts through the years, with acetate overlays to reveal inside activities.

Focus on Reading-Thinking Skills

Monitoring

Monitoring is checking to see what could be wrong, figuring out what to do about it, and then fixing mistakes. The mistakes could be in the content, the organization, the format or the mechanics of a passage. There are also mistakes that students make as they read. In reading, as in writing, students must become editors, examining works for accuracy and meaning. Develop this editorial viewpoint by teaching students to ask themselves questions such as:

- Does this make sense?
- Am I right?
- What does the author mean?
- Is this in order?
- What is missing in this sentence?
- Is this the correct spelling for this meaning?

To monitor well, students must recognize when they do not understand the material and be alert as to the cause. Is it the text or the reading of it?

Strategy—Description

Read a short description of a vivid physical scene to the class. History texts or biographies are a good source. Have students listen with their eyes closed, then illustrate what they have heard. Read the passage again while they listen and check their drawings. Afterward, encourage the students to compare their illustrations, discuss the differences and refer back to the passage for verification.

If the passage has an illustration, students can also compare their own to the text illustration. Ask them to look particularly for things they included that were not in the text illustration, but that made the written description more vivid.

The aim of this strategy is to hone students' ability to visualize what they listen to or read in a passage to assist with monitoring.

It appears that it is not a question of whether poor readers can image, but one which examines whether they can use this imagery to comprehend abstract concepts or make inferences.
Diane Truscott et al., educators and researchers

Strategy—Oops! What's Going On?

"Okay, hockey fans ... the commentator is getting excited! The centre speeds across the *red and* blue line, then slams on the brakes, spraying a shower of *ice chips and gravy* into the air. He hears his left-winger calling for the *middle* puck. He passes it off, then makes a break for the net. Oops! Did I hear correctly? Does he know how to play the game?"

Challenge your Info-Kids to detect the errors in the commentary. Too easy? Then try this one—have them read it rather than listen. Still too easy? Trios of students can take selections from information books, substituting errors for others to edit. Or, to make it even harder, students can develop their own commentaries to try tricking their peers' editing skills.

The aim of this strategy is for students to improve their editing ability by making sure the meaning of what they listen to, read or write is clear.

Focus on Research-Project Skills

Beyond Spelling

Of course, proofreading for mechanical errors has to be done before a research project is presented. However, there are bigger issues in editing than spelling that should be brought to the attention of students.

Organization is one such issue, one that shouldn't present too much trouble if early on the topics and facts within the project were categorized and sequenced in some logical order and checked for missing elements. Sometimes just listing the headings will help make the organization visible and obvious.

Reader understanding is another issue to consider when editing. Are there simply too many inferences for the reader to make? Are there too many gaps for the reader to fill in? A good idea is to get someone who hasn't encountered the project before to read or listen to. They will quickly notice any existing gaps.

A third editing issue is voice. This is perhaps the hardest of the three, but basically it implies that the person who wrote the piece is recognizable behind the words. Having two students interview the research project creator allows that individual to get an oral feel for the topic before writing.

Strategy—Is This Correct?

How do we know that the illustrations in books give a correct interpretation of the times? Certainly not from the romanticized generalities of hastily illustrated scenes. Encourage students to use *Castle Diary: The Journal of Tobias Burgess, Page* as a benchmark. Filled with expressive, large-nosed characters in various vignettes, the illustrations are packed with accurate details. How do other books compare? Consider adult books with photos of original paintings, tapestries and interiors for comparison. Put your editing skills to work—not just on text—but on illustrations too!

Teacher Realities

Some Info-Kids learn best in a visual manner, but the fact is that most classroom instruction is done orally. Research has repeatedly shown that two-thirds of the talk done in classrooms is done by teachers. We depend on talk to communicate our instruction, ignoring—to their detriment—the visual and tactile learners in our classrooms. Instead of repeating a direction three different times, begin using a different mode, perhaps by representing it physically, or especially for visual learners, in showing what you intend in some visual way.

...write the article—and rewrite it and rewrite until it says what you want to say about the subject in the way you want to say it. Now you're on your way to becoming a nonfiction writer!

James Cross Giblin, children's author quoted in Flora Wyatt

CHAPTER 13

Info-Kids Who Have Novel Perspectives

Charlotte's Web is about the life cycle of a pig! Right?

Characteristics

- Find no appeal in an imaginary world
- Focus on the facts in fiction books
- Relate best to stories about real people, places and things
- Seek out real-life adventures and documentaries

Resources for Success

- Biographies and autobiographies
- Historical fiction
- Diaries
- Journals
- Historical picture books
- Natural history accounts

Many Info-Kids who are reluctant readers do not see the value of reading because reading for them has always equaled stories. Too often we teachers focus on what we are personally interested in—usually fiction. This results in years of emphasis on stories in the primary grades in particular, and little heed to the nonfiction many kids are more interested in.

Info-Kids often have a different slant on how they imagine or think through things in their heads. When forced to read fiction, they focus on the background knowledge and the facts which set the context for the story, rather than on the tale itself. It is for the real things, rather than for what happens to imaginary people, that they read. Hence the appeal of biographies, autobiographies and documentaries, which are about what really happened. These students can also be caught in the lure of reality-based and technically-accurate science fiction, and the interesting facts in some fiction books. It is through introducing to them to such resources that they can be led to see some value in fiction.

Meet the Info-Kids

Roger—Bats about Bats!

Roger loves bats! In fact, he is quite mad about them. He loves to read about them but has difficulty getting down to work on any topic except bats! He has read all the books he can get his hands on, but still wants more. He even wants to build bat houses for the school so everyone can see real live bats.

Fortunately for him, his family went to Chautauqua, south of Buffalo in New York State, for a holiday. He was in heaven! Each evening, hundreds of bats came forth from under the eaves of the old Victorian houses. The public library had a lot of serious bat books and conservation officers gave weekly bat talks. Roger dramatically increased his knowledge and interest. Occasionally he went missing at night, but his family always found him, binoculars at the ready, observing the brown bats.

Luckily for Roger, the librarian introduced him to Kenneth Oppel's novel *Silverwing.* This is a fast-paced adventure about a young bat named Shade, who gets separated from his colony during the fall migration south to Hibernaculum. Roger was hooked! One could say he went batty over this novel! Previously he would not read novels at all, but with his experiential background and knowledge of bats, he was able to read this one with great depth and insight.

Just as Shade lacked self esteem in the beginning of the book, the many hair-raising experiences he had helped him to realize his uniqueness and valuable qualities. So it has been for Roger, as he has gradually evolved into a bat expert. Realizing that bats do not see colors, he insists on dressing accordingly. Although Roger does own a magnificent black cape, unlike the young girl in Sarah Withrow's *Bat Summer,* he does not believe he is a bat!

Matt—Many Men Read Differently

Matt is a keen sports player, as well as very artistic. He is not greatly intrigued by novels—it is like "pulling hen's teeth," but he will look at one if he will learn something or if it is on a topic that he is interested in at the moment. Fortunately, his dad has always taken a great interest in reading to him. Being a scientist, he has varied interests, and, consequently, his reading choices are usually nonfiction items, such as biographies, scientific theories and historical perspectives. He does occasionally read science fiction or fact-based fiction, so has enjoyed reading some novels with his son.

A favorite for both of them was E.B. White's *Stuart Little.* In reading this novel, they discussed the migratory habits of birds and the reasons why Stuart "went north" to find Margola, among other factual considerations. In sharp contrast, when Matt's mom read this same book to a younger brother, they talked about how Stuart might feel when his "date" went so wrong. After feeling all of Stuart's pain and disappointment, they stopped to discuss it and link it to their own disappointments.

It would never have occurred to his mother to discuss the scientific facts that underpin the novel. Yet, it is precisely these scientific facts that intrigue Matt so much and give him entrance into the narrative mode.

Focus on Interests

Stories Are Often Based on Facts

Info-Kids are, all too often, used to getting their information from a limited number of sources. They do not realize that all the resources available to them contain facts to some degree. Not valuing narrative accounts, they need to be encouraged to see that stories about real people, in particular, are based on facts, and indeed, that fiction writers frequently use true information in which to site their stories.

Strategy—Silent Flyers of the Night

There may be nothing as guaranteed to capture the attention of Info-Kids as the swooping of bats just after sunset, but many teachers will find it a challenge to snare them in a fantasy novel. Kenneth Oppel's *Silverwing* is more than just a migration story, laced as it is with danger and high drama. Info-Kids will get turned on to the tale because there are so many intriguing facts about bats cleverly intertwined with the narrative. A skillful teacher will interrupt the reading,

Fiction contains more truth than nonfiction.
Marion Crook, writer

talk about the concepts presented, challenge students to read between the lines and, as a fellow learner, review what has been found out about bats.

This novel allows for endless questions to be asked. Many could focus on scientific facts, such as:

- How do bats find things or locate things (echolocation)?
- Why do bats emit high-pitched sounds?
- How do bats use their wings for flying, for eating, for warmth, and for cooling down?
- How does the structure of their wings aid bats?
- What are the safe places to rest and roost which offer protection?
- What do bats eat anyway?

More complex questions could delve into the mistrust portrayed in the story among the birds, beasts and bats. For example:

- Could this be similar to prejudice and misunderstandings among humans?
- How do cults and mob mentality evolve?
- Who's got the power?

The aim of this strategy is to assist Info-Kids to realize that many novels are based on and contain many facts within the plot. Facts are indeed crucial to the successful exploits of the characters. Once this has been discovered, we can provide an opportunity for the power of story to embrace Info-Kids.

Strategy—It's My Life!

Preparing personal time lines can provide the first step in appreciating biographies. Invite your students to create a list of ten important happenings in their lives, and to plot these on a time line. Follow this up by having the students ask their parents and then grandparents to do the same. One thing that is immediately recognizable is the changing length of time covered on the lists and the types of happenings each chooses to list.

Favorite Bat Titles
- *Bat* by Caroline Arnold
- *Bat Loves the Night* by Nicola Davies
- *Bats: Night Fliers* by Betsy Maestro
- *The Fascinating World of Bats* by Marias Angels Julivert
- *What Is a Bat?* by Bobbie Kalman and Heather Levigne

Favorite Famous People Bios

- *Alexander Graham Bell: An Inventive Life* by Elizabeth MacLeod
- *The Amazing Life of Benjamin Franklin* by James Cross Giblin
- *Bull's Eye: A Photobiography of Annie Oakley* by Sue Macy
- *Gandhi* by Demi
- *Hatshepsut: His Majesty, Herself* by Catherine M. Andronik
- *Leonardo da Vinci* by Diane Stanley
- *Lucy Maud Montgomery: A Writer's Life* by Elizabeth MacLeod
- *Meet Christopher Columbus* (Landmark Books) by James T. DeKay
- *Starry Messenger: A Book Depicting the Life of a Famous Scientist, Mathematician, Astronomer, Philosopher and Physicist, Galileo Galilei* by Peter Sis

After all, there's a story to everything. The task of the nonfiction writer is to find the story—the narrative line that exists in nearly every subject.

Russell Freedman, writer quoted in Evelyn Freeman

Strategy—Introducing ME!

Invite students to create a home page about themselves. Suggest that they check in with the geocities site (www.geocities.yahoo.com) and design it for the Internet. Need some ideas? It is easy to search the geocities site to find out what others have done for themselves. Once a page is developed, students can get it printed and place it on a classroom bulletin board. Tell students to make certain to include a scanned photo, a short self-description, a past history and a welcome message. It is not absolutely necessary to post it on the Internet.

Focus on Resources

The Narrative-Fact Connection

While some information books include an element of story, there are various narratives that are particularly good at including facts. These books include journals, diaries, novels, mysteries and selected poetry. Narrative books based on facts, unlike nonfiction books, are intended as stories, but include real facts. This type of writing is very valuable as it gives a context for the facts presented. It situates facts in real-life settings so that students, Info-Kids in particular, learn not just lists of isolated facts but the connections between facts and people, facts and time, and indeed, facts and life.

Boys won't sit and listen to a story? Nonsense—it depends on the story. An underlying truism is that boys like narratives laced with facts. Thus, it behooves teachers to link such novels and stories with information books if the adventure is to be successful. For example, Lynn Reid Banks's overwhelming popular novel *Harry the Poisonous Centipede: A Story to Make You Squirm,* although appealing for the information she has woven into the plot, can be enhanced by sharing it with a nonfiction title such as Christina Coster-Longman's *Creepy Crawlies.* Through experiencing this novel, Info-Kids can find out about the anatomy of the centipede, and glean that it cannot survive in water and that it is aware of us because of the vibrations of our movements. Looking at close-up photographs in an information book and reading the descriptions will add a new dimension of reality.

Strategy—Diaries, Journals and Logbooks

Diaries, journals and logbooks are the perfect place to start in introducing narrative to Info-Kids as these books are about the real lives of real people, and are full of real facts and action. Historical fiction titles particularly rely on factual details to enhance the setting, time and action. Try some of these:

Nonfiction can be told in a narrative voice and still maintain its integrity. The art of fiction is making up facts; the art of nonfiction is using facts to make up a form.

Jean Fritz, children's author quoted in Evelyn Freeman

- Bouchard, David. *The Journal of Etienne Mercier.* The journal of an 1853 Hudson Bay man, writer and artist, describing a journey from Fort Victoria to the Queen Charlotte Islands by schooner. CD of journal included.
- Caslell, Maryanne. *Pioneer Girl.* Based on original 1887 letters of a young girl's experience arriving with her family on the Canadian prairies.
- Chorlton, Windsor. *Woolly Mammoth: Life, Death and Rediscovery.* Join a team of researchers as it travels to Siberia in search of a frozen mammoth.
- Greenwood, Barbara. *Gold Rush Fever: A Story of the Klondike, 1898.* Appealing short stories, diaries and background on the lure of the Yukon.

Students really enjoy reading historical fiction when it is correlated with social studies themes. They get very excited when they can make connections between the content we are studying and what is in their novel.

Margaret, teacher

- Manson, Ainslie. *House Calls: The True Story of a Pioneer Doctor.* The life of a doctor when a house call could mean a several-day trip.
- Meyer, Carolyn. *Mary, Bloody Mary* (Young Royals). The daughter of Henry VII, Mary Tudor, becomes a servant in her own home—a riveting read.
- Morton, Alexandra. *In the Company of Whales: From the Diary of a Whale Watcher.* Join one of the leading researchers on orcas.
- Whiteley, Opal. *Only Opal: The Diary of a Young Girl.* The moving diary of an Oregon frontier child of the early 1900s during her fifth and sixth year of life.

Favorite Diaries

- *Anastasia: The Last Grand Duchess* (The Royal Diaries) by Carolyn Meyer
- *Cleopatra VII: Daughter of the Nile* (The Royal Diaries) by Kristina Gregory
- *Elizabeth I: Red Rose of the House of Tudor* (The Royal Diaries) by Kathryn Lasky
- *The Gold Rush* by Ian and Susan Wilson
- *Orphan at My Door: The Home Child Diary of Victoria Cope* (Dear Canada) by Jean Little
- *A Prairie as Wide as the Sea: The Immigrant Diary of Ivy Weatherall* (Dear Canada) by Sarah Ellis
- *The Shaman's Nephew: A Life in the Far North* by Simon Tookoome, with Sheldon Oberman

---

Strategy—Two-Minute Mysteries

Many students are keen fans of mystery stories and Info-Kids can enjoy digging out the facts that give clues to solving them. Although they may love reading them, the challenge in using facts comes when students have to write their own short mystery story.

As many schools have their own Web sites, including many classroom sites, have the students post their stories online. Then parents and friends can log on, read the mystery, and comment directly to the author. When this happens, the time spent devising the mystery and writing it becomes immaterial.

Try these to get your mystery readers/writers going:

- Ardagh, Philip. *Ancient Greece* (History Detectives). It looks just like a fact-filled picture account of life during the times, however, open the sealed envelope to reveal the mystery "Death at the Theatre." You'll have to find the clues in the book to solve the mystery. This series also features *Ancient Egypt, The Aztecs* and *The Romans.*
- Bowers, Vivien. *Crime Science.* How to use science to catch the nasty guys.
- Golden, Christopher. *The 10-Minute Detective: 25 Scene-of-the-Crime Mystery Puzzles You Can Solve Yourself.* These will challenge you!
- Jackson, Donna M. *The Bone Detectives: How Forensic Anthropologists Solve Crimes and Uncover Mysteries of the Dead.* The bones tell it all.

?

So, you know all about Monet's garden, but what is the subject of his 1877 painting, "The Gare St.-Lazare?"

Just what the title says—the St.-Lazare train station.

- Nilsen, Anna. *Art Fraud Detective.* Readers are tipped off by a guard that several paintings have been sold on the black market and forgeries are now hanging in the gallery. Thirty-four paintings are presented. Only four are authentic. A magnifying glass is enclosed to assist in the investigation.
- Spalding, Andrea and David. *The Lost Sketch: Unlock the Mystery Found in the Boxcar* (Adventure.Net). Two kids find a painting in an old boxcar—could it be valuable? Information inserts throughout the novel add to the intrigue.
- Sukach, Jim. *Clever Quicksolve Whodunit Puzzles: Mini-Mysteries for You to Solve.* Dr. Quicksolve and his son solve 38 terse (1-2 page) cases.

Strategy—Poetry? With Information? You Must Be Joking!

It's not a joke! Just as journals, novels and mysteries can depend on facts to give details, so too can poetry. What is different in poetry is the particular attention to the specificity, the beauty and the emotional power of the words and phrases used. Poetry offers the chance for investigating questions such as:

- Why does this particular word or phrase get the meaning across better than another?
- Why does this particular word or phrase convey the impression required?
- Why does this word or phrase, rather than that one, illustrate the fact so well?
- How do the facts assist the creation of the visual impression?

Some factual poetry books to start with include:

- Frank, John. *The Tomb of the Boy King.* Poetic account of the discovery of the tomb of Tutankhamen.
- Thayer, Ernest Lawrence. *Casey at the Bat.* Comparing this edition to others will reveal the richness of the visual interpretation in the illustrations of Christopher Bing.
- Yolen, Jane. *Sacred Places.* A certain reverence emits from the pages as words and illustrations combine to share about our holy places: Delphi, Copan, WailingWall, Easter Island, Stonehenge, Uluru, Mecca … A splendid opportunity is created to extend the concepts by gleaning facts about the geographical settings and mythologies from relevant resources.

Focus on Reading-Thinking Skills

Appreciative Reading

One aspect of critical reading is appreciative reading; the aesthetic, emotive, personal feeling that is generated by characteristics of good writing. This is an aspect of reading that Info-Kids often avoid by preference and leave to fiction readers.

Yet, playing on their pragmatism, particularly in making decisions about the values stated in texts and distinguishing fantasy from reality, they can be induced to savor at least some aspects of appreciative reading. Ask questions such as:

- How do you feel when ...?
- What would you do ...?

Give us books we can read and that don't put us to sleep.

Laura Robb,
reading educator

- What words made you feel, see, smell, taste, hear ...?
- Do you know someone like ...?

Strategy—Make Me a Hero

Kids love a hero—someone who rights wrongs, slays the dragons and saves the weak. Heroes are our idealized best. What qualities do we value? Why could it be that we honor goodness, power, beauty, pleasure, truth, order and worth? What do we want of our best?

Brainstorm a list of "hero" traits. Ask students to remember and discuss specific heroes they have read about in books, or seen on TV, in movies, or in video games. Talk about real life heroes in newspapers, news reports and in their own lives. Compare the traits of the story characters with those of real-life heroes using a Venn diagram. Which ones are common to all? Have students name those "hero" characteristics we most value and discuss why they are important.

The aim of this strategy is to make students aware of and to appreciate the qualities we value in people. This, in turn, can help them understand why we include what we value in stories.

Strategy—How Are You "Peeling"?

With a group of students, summarize the critical events from a story, biography or documentary. Then, together, discuss the emotions felt while reading each event. Together, create a graph of the events in sequence on one side and of the range of feelings felt on the other. Next, ask students to individually graph their emotional responses to the events.

Compare differences in the individual graphs about the same story. Here is a chance to discuss the different emotions each of us feels even though we are reading the same text, and how we come to those differences through our background experiences.

A good visual resource that shows moods and expressions is *How Are You Peeling? Foods with Moods* by Saxton Freymann and Joost Elffers. This dramatic photographic interpretation of changes in mood is evidenced by the shapes of various vegetables. Info-Kids will eagerly swarm to their neighborhood grocery store to look for further examples, and to produce their own more complicated glossary.

The aim of this strategy is for all of us to see how events in the story, and the author's writing skill, elicit emotional responses in each of us that are sometimes very different.

Focus on Research-Project Skills

The One-Minute Presentation

An important aspect of any student research project is learning how to present the information to the class. It takes courage to do a presentation—this is why public speaking is the number one fear of adults. Let your students have fun while they undertake short, one-minute speeches to practise being on their feet in front of an audience, talking in public, and presenting their information in a way that others can easily understand.

Strategy—Ham and Cheese It Up

Using an information book of interest, encourage students to find three important facts to present. Then, have them use a sandwich format to organize their presentation: A short, snappy, one-sentence introduction/ the three facts/ a short, to-the-point conclusion. Give the students 10 to 15 minutes to do the research and put their notes on index cards, then they are ready to begin presenting.

Variations on this strategy—on an environmental theme—could include: making an appeal to save an endangered species; encouraging people to do something to save the environment; or requesting parents to write to a legislative member to save the habitat of a species.

The aim of this strategy is to allow students to gain confidence in public speaking by repeated practice sessions on topics of their choice. Of course, you can't say a lot in one minute, therefore, as confidence grows, gradually increase the time upwards to three to five minutes.

Strategy—We Interrupt This Program

Using a computer for formatting, have the students prepare a one-minute news broadcast on a current topic of interest. Encourage them to study news anchors to see how they read their scripts and look directly into the television camera. What news could be so urgent or of such a serious nature that a sports program or movie would be interrupted? How would the announcer sound? How would he/she most effectively present the information?

Usually a particular book is what triggers reluctant readers. I keep suggesting/giving/showing/reading different genres until they find one that interests them.

Bonnie, teacher

Teacher Realities

Most Info-Kids like to think about real things, not imaginary ones. When they are forced to read fiction, they have a differing view of story in that they seek out the information, the history, and the facts. They are not concerned with the possible themes and morals, but with what, and how, things really happened. Any connections you can make to reality help expand their horizons with fiction, hence the importance of such resources as biographies, autobiographies, journals and diaries.

Part C: The Satisfaction of Working With Info-Kids

CHAPTER 14

Are They Reading?

Ultimately, all testing is subjective.

The ultimate question is always: "Are the kids reading any better?" For us as teachers, the most useful evaluation is that which looks at readers individually and tells us how they are doing and what would help. But any evaluation done in the classroom should be quick and efficient and not interrupt instruction. It should also be based on instructional objectives and become ongoing. As professionals, our aim is to find, or create, the best test for our situation.

Reading tests of various types and intents abound—some useful, some not; some formal, others informal; some published, and some teacher-made. One type tells us how students stand in relation to others across the district, province or nation. These are usually formal published tests of the multiple choice variety and they allow us to tell if our students are reading above, below or at the same level as the kids in the school down the street. Another type tells us our students' grade level in reading. These tests are also usually formal published tests that give us scores in comprehension, vocabulary and word identification, or sometimes just grade levels. They are often used for grade placement.

A third type, diagnostic reading tests, are the most useful for teachers of Info-Kids who are reluctant to read. Diagnostic tests give an idea of students' strengths and weaknesses in reading. The most familiar diagnostic tests for most teachers are Informal Reading Inventories (IRIs) which require students to read a passage then answer questions. Some include retelling after reading, cloze, graded word lists, etc. The biggest problem with IRIs is that they must be done one-on-one and so are time consuming. No matter how valuable they are in understanding readers' strengths and weaknesses, we have trouble finding the time in an already too busy day to administer them. What we need are types of diagnostic tests that allow us to make quick and efficient yet accurate judgments, and to get on with the job—tests that allow us to do them as we are teaching.

Observation

The real act of discovery consists not in finding new lands but in new eyes.

Marcel Proust, French novelist

Observation allows us to do this. It can be quickly and easily used in the classroom while students are actually reading. Observation has the advantage of being done in snippets of time, one bit today, one bit tomorrow. Our daily, but often unvoiced, intuitions about instruction are based on observation.

Effective observation includes two important parts. The first part is in the actual watching, in which we must look closely for clues. Watching allows us to describe what is happening and to see patterns that occur over and over again. To make the most of our watching, we must note down what we see. These anecdotal notes kept over a few months show the patterns and are a good source for writing up student reports. The second part is taking the time to make sense of what we see so that we know what to do. This means looking over our notes, sorting the behaviors identified into categories (patterns), going back and watching to see if the patterns emerge again, and finally, making decisions about why they are happening and what to do to improve reading.

There are many ways of directing observation. One is random; just watching what goes on during literacy activities in the classroom with no particular goal. After enough time, we begin seeing the same things happening over and over again and can label those patterns. Another type of observation is based on watching using a time schedule. For example, we might observe for 30 seconds every 5 minutes during uninterrupted sustained silent reading. Or, our observation might be based on a particular behavior we noticed; identifying how often, or who, where or when it happens. In this case, we might choose to observe which books are chosen from the classroom library. A fourth observation method is using checklists to note instances of specific behaviors.

A constant danger is that our inherent biases will affect our observations. The thing we must always do is to try to observe with an open eye and an active ear. Thus, we must continually question the accuracy of the information we have gathered—are we seeing what is really there? We must also question what we have focused on—do we only see one thing and ignore others? And, finally, we must question what we believe about reading and writing—do we believe that the way we teach reading is right and every other way wrong?

Checklists

One of the best supports we know for observation are checklists. Checklists are an easy way to guide observation and remind us of what is worth looking for. Having checklists around to use every month or so reminds us that we need to observe students as they work. Yet, a checklist is helpful only if the behaviors it directs us to observe are important to understanding a student's reading strengths and weaknesses, which can lead us to more pertinent instruction.

Some of the most useful checklists are ones we develop ourselves. But be careful—there is a danger with self-made checklists in that they may act as blinders producing tunnel vision. We must always be alert, watching for significant behaviors to add.

We need to evaluate the value of all checklists to make sure the statements used within them relate to specific reading behaviors. They should be well organized and specifically focused rather than jump all over the reading landscape. For example, questions about attitude, phonics and critical reading abilities all on one checklist make the list so general that it leads us nowhere, confusing rather than clarifying. This type of checklist can leave us where we started—still confused. The most useful checklist focuses on a particular area we want to evaluate at a given time. The following are a few sample checklists related to some of the themes explored in this book.

Direct observation is an important source of information. Our lives are filled with hundreds of processes occurring simultaneously at any given moment within a few feet of us.

Donald Graves,
educator and researcher

Interest Checklist

An interest checklist is intended to find out about students' reading likes and dislikes, to tap into their interests, and to help identify what topics and genres they may be most willing to read. Here is a list of sample questions you can ask to get students talking about their interests:

According to one study, the top ten reading preferences for grade six students are: 1—scary books or story collections; 2—cartoons and comics; 3—popular magazines; 4—sports; 5—drawing books; 6—cars and trucks; 7—animals; 8—series; 9—funny novels; 10—books written mostly for adults. What is most available in schools? "Good" novels.

Jo Worthy et al.,
educators and researchers

- What is the best book ever read to you?
- What is the best book you ever read?
- What are your favorite hobbies?
- What do you like to do after school?
- What are some of your favorite movies?
- What television programs do you like best?
- What are your favorite Web sites?
- What school subjects do you find most interesting?
- What sports do you like best?
- What are your favorite pets?
- What kinds of art activities do you like?
- Where would you go if you could take a trip?

From the answers to these questions, we should get an idea of what students' interests are and, from that, be able to choose suitable materials and activities. (Adapted from Paul Burns, et al.)

Nonverbal Behaviors Checklist

This type of checklist looks at nonverbal reading behaviors during actual reading. It gives clues about nonverbal behaviors that indicate whether readers are involved and interested in what they are reading, or not. For example, does the reader (or, instead, do you):

- Pick up literacy materials (book, paper, etc.)?
- Replace materials (book, etc.) when finished reading?
- Hold the book? With two hands?
- Keep track in the book of reading place?
- Turn the page?
- Position the literacy materials for convenience of reading?
- Lean toward the materials?
- Choose materials?
- Appear engaged and actively involved?

If readers show most of these behaviors, they are reading something that interests them, are comfortable in the reading situation, and most likely are reading at their independent level. If instead, we are doing these behaviors, the student is probably disinterested, avoiding the situation and not paying attention. Try to keep reading in the reader's hands. (Adapted from Mary Dayton-Sakari)

Verbal Behaviors Checklist

This type of checklist looks at verbal behaviors mature readers show as they read when interested in what they are reading and while interacting with others. For example, does the reader (or do you):

- Initiate questions?
- Make connections to background knowledge?
- Clarify information?
- Demonstrate meaning?
- Develop passage structure through voice?
- Draw attention to illustrations?
- Extend other students' responses?
- Extend vocabulary?
- Inform?
- Point out detail?
- Narrate text and or pictures?
- Praise?
- Point out text features?

If readers show these behaviors, then they are involved in what they are reading. If it is us showing these behaviors, and not the reader, we likely have a disinterested, non-attending, non-understanding reader. Try to become an active listener rather than the "teller" in reading. (Adapted from Janell Klesius and Priscilla Griffith)

Reading-Thinking Processes Checklist

This type of checklist shows how students think as they read. It tells us if they are able to use the different ways we think effectively when reading. We know students think in different ways for different purposes during reading just as they do in any other learning. When we read, we reconstruct and regulate our understanding of the text and the words. We reconstruct by associating, inferring and predicting, analyzing and synthesizing. We regulate by monitoring. Looking at students' reading-thinking processes helps us decide what kind of instruction would be most helpful. You may wish to consider the following questions for each reading-thinking process explored in this book.

Associating

Does the student:

- Answer vocabulary questions?
- Group like items together?
- Create categories and category titles for information details?
- Match the correct sounds and letters in miscues?

If students don't show they can associate easily, instruction should include strategies similar to the reading-thinking strategies suggested in chapter 7. Try these or other activities that help them make connections between words or meanings, and create categories.

Predicting/Inferring

Does the student:

- Answer inference and prediction questions?
- Use the passage and background knowledge to guess what comes next?

Where the teacher's expertise really counts ... is in knowing what the child is going to want ... the more they can allow themselves to hold back and allow the student to do his own learning, the more effective, and better judged will be their interventions.

Asher Cashan,
reading educator and researcher

- Use the passage and background knowledge to produce inferred information appropriate to the passage?
- Fill in cloze blanks with words that are meaningful, rather than words that are not meaningful to the passage?
- Use miscues that are meaningful to the passage rather than nonsense ones?

If students show they have trouble predicting and inferring, strategies like those in chapters 9 and 11 should help. Try these or other activities that ask students to make educated guesses about what will happen next and to fill in gaps left by the author.

Analyzing

Does the student:

- Answer factual questions?
- Produce the exact, or almost the exact words and thoughts, from the passage in a retelling?
- Use one half or more of the letters from the original word in a miscue?
- Use the beginning, middle and end part of the word in a miscue? (A developmental progression is to use the beginning, add the end, then the middle letters.)
- Use single letters or clusters from the original word in a miscue? (A developmental progression is to use single letters, then clusters.)
- Produce nonsense words rather than real words as miscues?

If students cannot analyze easily, which is not often the case with Info-Kids who love knowing facts, try strategies like exploring the 5 Ws—who, what, where, when, why, how—or newspaper leads. These activities require finding details and picking out the most important ones.

Synthesizing

Does the student:

- Answer relationship questions?
  - cause-effect
  - sequence
  - comparison
  - contrast
- Produce information from the passage that has been combined or reformed into his/her own words?
- Produce paraphrased and summarized information?
- Answer summary questions?
- Produce a main idea or theme?
- Try to sound out unknown words or blends?

If they show trouble synthesizing, strategies like those in chapters 6 and 8 should help. Try these or other activities that help students paraphrase or summarize, and those that help them understand relationships like sequence, cause and effect, comparison and contrast.

He found out he was a better reader than a rival and began volunteering for oral reading.

Russell, teacher

Monitoring

Does the student:

- Correct answers to questions?
- Produce repetitions, corrections or additions to the text?
- Make corrections, erasures or regressions in reading while doing a cloze exercise?
- Pause and notice there are miscues?
- Correct or attempt to correct any of the miscues?

If students show they have trouble monitoring, strategies like those in chapter 12 will help. Try these or other activities that require editing and thinking about how to figure out what to do if something is incorrect.

Checklists take little time and give a good enough idea of problems so that we can focus our instruction to help struggling Info-Kids become better readers. As with any test, however, be aware of how and why you use checklists. Used carefully, they work.

Interpreting Observations and Reporting to Parents

The point of observation, checklists or any other diagnostic evaluation is to gain facts about kids' reading that can aid in planning further instruction and reporting to parents. The above four types of checklists give an idea of what students believe about their own reading, what they might be interested in reading about, what they communicate nonverbally as they read, what they can discuss as they read, and finally—perhaps most important for instruction—which thinking processes they feel most comfortable with as they read.

The two most common questions parents ask about their child's reading are: "How is he/she doing?" and "What can I do to help?" We need to be able to answer these questions in a very practical manner. Observation checklists can help us give useful and understandable answers.

From the information we gain from an interest checklist, we can inform parents as to the reading materials that would most interest their child and keep him or her most interested in reading.

From a nonverbal behaviors checklist, we can point out to parents if their child is involved with and manipulating reading materials, or if the child leaves the "touching" to others. We can help parents think about who is handling the books being read at home and encourage them to give that role of being in charge of the materials to their child, thereby encouraging more student control of the act of reading.

From a verbal behaviors checklist, we can talk about the kinds of questions and discussion points about the book's content that parents can initiate to encourage a better understanding of books read at home.

And, last, but we think most useful, the reading-thinking checklist can enable you to call attention to the kinds of thinking that are easiest for the child, but more important for growth, the kinds of thinking that give the child trouble. Using this checklist, you should get an idea of whether a student is strong or

A student entered my classroom on opening day with the statement, "I hate to read and there isn't anything you can do about it!" At the end of the year, he came up to me and asked. "You aren't going to finish our book are you?" When I responded that I wouldn't, he asked to take it home for the weekend so he could complete it. And he did!

Janet, teacher

weak at analyzing, synthesizing, associating, predicting and inferring, and monitoring. Usually they are good at one or two and can use help in the others. In fact, we have found, when analyzing for reading-thinking processes in a clinic situation with struggling readers, that there are some common patterns that show up over and over.

The most common pattern is one in which the reader is good at analyzing and poor at predicting and inferring. Most Info-Kids have this kind of pattern. This means that these kids can pick out facts and have a decent grasp of phonics, but they cannot use the book or their world knowledge to help them understand the material or even individual words in the material.

Most Common Pattern for Info-Kids

predicting/inferring	analyzing
WEAK in comprehension and word identification	STRONG in comprehension and word identification

The kinds of things you can tell parents that they can do at home to help children with this pattern are to:

- Encourage them to ask "why" questions about what is being read
- Talk about what might happen next
- Talk about what the author left out or really meant
- Try to use the meaning around a word to help figure out miscues

The second most common pattern is a cross pattern, one in which the reader is good at predicting and inferring in comprehension, but weak at using predicting and inferring in word identification. Plus, this type of reader is strong in analyzing in figuring out words but weak in analyzing in comprehension. This means the reader depends on background knowledge to understand and cannot pick out the important facts in the material to give a grounding to what he guesses. It means the reader doesn't know how to use the meaning around a word to help figure out words, but depends on phonics instead. This child is often a word-by-word reader, with little understanding of what has been read.

Cross Pattern

predicting/inferring	analyzing
STRONG in comprehension WEAK in word identification	WEAK in comprehension STRONG in word identification

Parents can help at home by discussing the facts, finding the 5 Ws, and asking questions such as "Does that word make sense?"

The third pattern is one where the reader is good at predicting, but poor at analyzing. This type of reader depends on grasping knowledge from the whole and pays little attention to specifics. These kids are the dreamers, the fantasizers, and the very imaginative readers. Info-Kids are not as likely to show this pattern.

Least Common Pattern for Info-Kids

predicting/inferring	analyzing
STRONG in comprehension and word identification	WEAK in comprehension and word identification

Parents can help at home with these readers by helping them find facts and focusing on phonics.

In conjunction with, but independent of these three possible patterns in predicting/inferring vs. analysis, readers can be strong or weak at synthesizing. This means they can be good or poor at summarizing and paraphrasing, and finding relationships like cause and effect or sequences. They can also be strong or weak at monitoring. They can be good or poor at seeing and then correcting the mistakes they make in reading. Parents can help at home, if necessary, by discussing the main idea, theme or moral inherent in the material being read, talking about the order of events, making comparisons and showing contrasts. They can also assist by asking if the material and words read make sense and help figure out how to correct mistakes.

Whatever pattern readers show, whatever their strengths and weaknesses, whatever strategies and activities are used to bolster their weaknesses, there are some general things that both teachers and parents can do to make the reading situation more acceptable to a reader. We need to learn to be a silent partner by:

- Setting up a place to work that feels good
- Having an attitude that makes risk taking okay
- Seeking possibilities and not the one right answer
- Learning to ask "why" questions
- Making sure we understand the importance of always using materials that kids are interested in

It all focuses on building relationships. When you as a teacher show that you genuinely care through "actions," then students will risk and make an effort.

Bev, teacher

Using interests means the child will be much more likely to pay attention. No learning, about reading or otherwise, will happen unless the learner pays attention. Interest creates the desire to know, to learn and to apply oneself.

CHAPTER 15

Secrets of Success

You're never too old to be an Info-Kid!

As teachers it is our professional responsibility to continue to be active readers and active learners while we are influencing the lives of young people. Whether we like it or not, we are models of reading. We must aim to be models of not just fiction readers, but of information book readers as well.

It is important to feel the passion, catch the spirit and be consumed with wanting to find information about a topic of your own in order to understand Info-Kids. Consider the following to get you started.

Become a Fact Finder

The first step in becoming an Info-Kid is to make a list of what you are interested in right at this moment. Drawing a blank? It's okay! Here are a few guiding questions:

- What hobbies do you have?
- What TV programs do you watch?
- What types of books do you read?
- What sports do you play or watch?
- What types of materials do you read for directions or information?

Whether we have given release to our Info-Kid nature in the past or not, it is never too late. We just have to give ourselves "permission" to pursue something we've always wanted to do—in other words, to develop a passion. To do this, prioritize your list, starring those items that hold greater interest, and it will soon be obvious what you like to do. Once a decision has been made, it allows you to consider exploring a certain topic from a variety of approaches, and to determine your reading focus for the coming months.

What have you always wanted to read but never made time for? If you like to read historical mysteries or novels, you could get a good account of the times or a biography of a leader of the period to extend your appreciation of the facts incorporated by a writer into a text. Medieval mystery fans might even consider perusing some of the children's books referred to in Chapter 12. Just as we want

Info-Kids to have the freedom to consult adult references, so too should adults realize the value of consulting children's information books to obtain an essential broad overview of a topic. We guarantee that by doing this your conversational prowess at cocktail parties will improve impressively—to say nothing of at curriculum planning meetings!

Be an Info-Kid Model

Once we become as excited with our passions as Info-Kids are with theirs, whether it be orchids or Model 'A's, it becomes easier for us to understand how these kids operate, how they think and how they perceive the world. We'll be able to discover a new awareness of the world around us, exciting new resources to peruse, and easier ways to connect with kids that will renew our vigor. For example, we might give impromptu book talks or read snippets aloud to the class.

However, we need to remember to model not only our joy in the content, but also our own thinking as we undertake reading on a particular topic. Don't forget that we need to share the ideas we have discovered in a book, our personal research strategies, and our continuing approaches to our topic. Of course we have to be honest about both our successes and challenges in the maze of doing research, even noting dead ends.

We can do all this ourselves, but why not consider having your principal or teacher-librarian come to share favorite information books? Parents too may enjoy modeling their passion for particular topics and information resources.

It is crucial that we realize that our reading and commenting on nonfiction books shows that we value information resources, but more importantly, by valuing information, it strongly indicates that we value the Info-Kids in our class.

**Take charge
of your own literacy and teaching
Shape it
by your own hand and vision
Do not be swayed
by loud, insistent voices
Listen to and value your own voice
You are the teacher.**

*Regie Routman,
educator and researcher*

Tips for Engaging Info-Kids

Writing this book has been a long process, but an enjoyable one of revisiting our own experiences with Info-Kids, as well as consulting with teachers in the University of Victoria Reading Clinic and many classroom teacher colleagues. We have written of the ideas which have worked for all of us in our classrooms with students who certainly are Info-Kids—many of whom are reluctant readers and some that are not.

If we were asked to list those essential ideas that can lead to success with Info-Kids, we would have to state the following:

- We must accept information/nonfiction resources as legitimate literature. Nonfiction is not a second class citizen!
- We must accept the fact that Info-Kids will rarely get beyond their obsession with the facts.
- We must remember that one of the most valuable strategies for teachers is to read information/nonfiction books aloud in class.
- The only way to hook Info-Kids is through their interests, no matter what they are.
- No curriculum is perfect! Not everyone gets the same things from it anyway.
- A parallel curriculum offers connections to the Info-Kid.
- We learn to read by practising reading. Let Info-Kids practise through reading nonfiction.
- The Internet is really just a "cyberspace nonfiction book!"
- Information resources must be accurate and up to date—if not, discard them!
- We must let information resources do their work. Properly selected, they will intrigue.

There is no doubt that Info-Kids provide an immense challenge to the creativity, flexibility and originality of teachers. We can embrace this, or balk by insisting on conformity of everyone in the class, thereby risking disinterest, and thus creating more non-readers. It's up to us!

Professional References

Bamford, Rosemary, and Janice Kristo, eds. *Making Facts Come Alive: Choosing Quality Nonfiction Literature K-8.* Norwood, MA: Christopher-Gordon, 1998.

Burns, Paul, Betty Roe, and Elinor Ross. *Teaching Reading in Today's Elementary Schools.* 5th ed. Boston: Houghton Mifflin, 1992.

Carter, Betty, and Richard Abrahamson. "Castles to Colin Powell: The Truth about Nonfiction." In K. Beers and B. Samuels, eds., *Into Focus: Understanding and Creating Middle School Readers.* Norwood, MA: Christopher-Gordon, 1998, 313-332.

Cashan, Asher. "Who Teaches the Child to Read." In J. Merritt, ed., *New Horizons in Reading.* Newark, DE: IRA, 1976, 80-85.

Cassady, Judith. "Wordless Books: No-Risk Tools for Inclusive Middle-Grade Classrooms." *Journal of Adolescent & Adult Literacy,* 41, 6, 1998, 428-433.

Caswell, Linda, and Nell Duke. "Non-Narrative as a Catalyst for Literacy Development." *Language Arts,* 75, 2, 1998, 108-117.

Chambers, Aidan. *Introducing Books to Children.* 2nd ed. Boston: The Horn Book, 1983.

Cianciolo, Patricia J. *Informational Picture Books for Children.* American Library Association, 2000.

Crook, Marion. *Writing Books for Kids and Teens.* Vancouver, BC: Self Counsel Press, 1998.

Cullinan, Bernice, ed. *Fact and Fiction: Literature across the Curriculum.* Newark, DE: IRA, 1993.

Dayton-Sakari, Mary. "Struggling Readers Don't Work at Reading: They Just Get Their Teacher To!" *Intervention in School and Clinic,* 32 (5), 1997, 295-301.

Duthie, Christine. *True Stories: Nonfiction Literacy in the Primary Classroom.* Portland, MA: Stenhouse, 1996.

Fink, Rosalie. "Successful Dyslexics: A Constructivist Study of Passionate Interest Reading." *Journal of Adolescent & Adult Literacy,* 39, 4, 1995, 268-280.

Frank, Marjorie. *If You're Trying to Teach Kids How to Write ...* Nashville, TN: Incentive, 1995.

Freeman, Evelyn, and Diane Person, eds. *Using Nonfiction Trade Books in the Elementary Classroom: From Ants to Zeppelins.* NCTE, 1992.

Fry, Edward. *The Reading Teacher's Book of Lists.* 3rd ed. Englewood Cliffs, NJ: Prentice Hall, 1993.

Graves, Donald. *Investigate Nonfiction* (The Reading/Writing Teacher's Companion). Toronto, ON: Irwin/Portsmouth, NH: Heinemann, 1989.

Guthrie, John, and Ann McCann. "Characteristics of Classrooms That Promote Motivations and Strategies for Learning." In J. Guthrie and A. Wigfield, eds., *Reading Engagement: Motivating Readers through Integrated Instruction.* Newark, DE: IRA, 1997.

Harvey, Stephanie. *Nonfiction Matters: Reading, Writing and Research in Grades 3-8.* Portland, MA: Stenhouse, 1998.

Jobe, Ron, and Mary Dayton-Sakari. *Reluctant Readers: Connecting Students and Books for Successful Reading Experiences.* Markham, ON: Pembroke, 1999.

Klesius, Janell, and Priscilla Griffith. "Interactive Storybook Reading for At-Risk Learners." In R. Allington, ed., *Teaching Struggling Readers: Articles from the Reading Teacher.* Newark, DE: IRA, 1998.

McCormick, Sandra. *Instructing Students Who Have Literacy Problems.* 3rd ed. Englewood Cliffs, NJ: Prentice Hall, 1999.

McKenna, Michael, et al. "The Electronic Transformation of Literacy and Its Implications for the Struggling Reader." *Reading & Writing Quarterly,* 15, 2, 1999, 111-127.

Reuf, Kerry. *The Private Eye.* Seattle, WA: The Private Eye Project, 1996.

Riechel, Rosemarie. *Children's Nonfiction for Adult Information Needs.* North Haven, CT: Linnet, 1998.

Robb, Laura. "Helping Reluctant Readers Discover Books." *Book Links*, March, 1998, 51-53.

Routman, Regie. *Conversations: Strategies for Teaching, Learning and Evaluating.* Heinemann, 2000.

Skretta, John. "King's Works and the At-Risk Student." In Brenda M. Power, Jeffrey Wilhelm, and Kelly Chandler, eds., *Reading Stephen King.* Urbana, IL: National Council of Teachers of English, 1997.

Truscott, Diane, et al. "Poor Readers Don't Image, or Do They?" *Reading Research Report,* No. 38. Athens, GA: National Reading Research Center, 1995.

Worthy, Jo, et al. "What Johnny Likes to Read Is Hard to Find in School." *Reading Research Quarterly,* 34, 1, 1999, 12-27.

Wright, Cora. *Hot Links: Literature Links for the Middle School Curriculum.* Englewood, CO: Libraries Unlimited, 1998.

Wyatt, Flora, et al. *Popular Nonfiction Authors for Children: A Biographical and Thematic Guide.* Englewood, CO: Libraries Unlimited, 1998.

Info-Kid Resources

Adams, Simon. *World War II* (Eyewitness). Photographs by Andy Crawford. Dorling Kindersley, 2000.

Alles, Hemesh, illus. *Errata: A Book of Historical Errors*. Written by S.A.J. Wood. Green Tiger/Simon & Schuster, 1992.

Andronik, Catherine M. *Hatshepsut: His Majesty, Herself*. Illustrated by Joseph Daniel Fielder. Atheneum, 2001.

Angliss, Sarah. *Science Now*. Silver Dolphin, 2000

Ardagh, Philip. *Ancient Egypt* (History Detectives). Illustrated by Colin King. Peter Bedrick, 2000.

____ *Ancient Greece* (History Detectives). Illustrated by Colin King. Macmillan UK, 2000.

____ *Did Dinosaurs Snore? 100½ Questions about Dinosaurs Answered*. Faber & Faber, 2001.

Armstrong, Jennifer. *Shipwreck at the Bottom of the World: The Extraordinary True Story of Schackleton and the Endurance*. Crown, 1998.

Arnold, Caroline. *Bat*. Photographs by Richard Hewett. Morrow, 1996.

____ *Giant Shark: Megalodon, Prehistoric Super Predator*. Illustrated by Laurie Caple. Clarion, 2000.

____ *Lion*. Photographs by Richard Hewett. Morrow, 1995.

____ *Rhino*. Photographs by Richard Hewett. Morrow, 1995.

Ash, Russell. *Incredible Comparisons*. Dorling Kindersley, 1996.

____ *The Top 10 of Everything 2001*. Dorling Kindersley, 2001.

____ *Top 10 Quiz Book*. Dorling Kindersley, 2001.

Aulenbach, Nancy, and Hazel Barton. *Exploring Caves: Journeys into the Earth*. National Geographic, 2001.

Baggaley, Ann, ed. *Human Body*. Dorling Kindersley, 2001.

Bailey, Linda. *Adventures in Ancient Egypt*. Illustrated by Bill Slavin. Kids Can, 2000.

____ *Adventures with the Vikings* (Good Times Travel Agency). Illustrated by Bill Slavin. Kids Can, 2001.

Banks, Lynn Reid. *Harry the Poisonous Centipede: A Story to Make You Squirm*. Illustrated by Tony Ross. Avon, 1997.

Barnie, David. *Dictionary of Nature*. Dorling Kindersley, 1994.

Barrett, Paul. *Dinosaurs*. Illustrated by Raul Martin. National Geographic, 2001.

Bartholomew, Alan. *Electric Gadgets and Gizmos: Battery-Powered Buildable Gadgets That Go!* Kids Can, 1998.

Base, Graeme. *Animalia*. Viking Kestrel, 1986.

_____ *The Discovery of Dragons*. Elan/Penguin Australia, 1996.

Bathroom Readers' Institute. *Uncle John's All-Purpose Extra Strength Bathroom Reader*. Bathroom Readers' Press, 2000.

Baxter, Nicola. *Castle under Attack* (DK Readers: Lego). Dorling Kindersley, 2000.

_____ *Mission to the Arctic* (DK Readers: Lego). Illustrated by Roger Harris. Dorling Kindersley, 2000.

_____ *Rocket Rescue* (DK Readers: Lego). Illustrated by Julian Baum. Dorling Kindersley, 2000.

BBC Walking with Dinosaurs: 3D Dinosaurs. Dorling Kindersley, 1999.

Beecroft, Simon. S*uper Humans: A Beginner's Guide to Bionics* (Future Files). Copper Beech, 1998.

Benger, Michael, and Duane Raleigh. *Climbing Rock: Tools and Techniques*. Elk Mountain Press, 1995.

Berger, Melvin and Guilda. *Mummies of the Pharaohs: Exploring the Valley of the Kings*. National Geographic, 2001.

Bergin, Mark. *Castle* (Fast Forward). Scholastic Canada, 1999.

Biddle, Steve and Migumi. *Planet Origami: Cosmic Paper Folding for Kids*. Barron's, 1998.

Birkinshaw, Marie. *Race for Survival* (DK Readers: Lego). Illustrated by Roger Harris. Dorling Kindersley, 2000.

_____ *Secret at Dolphin Bay* (DK Readers: Lego). Illustrated by Jason Cook. Dorling Kindersley, 2000.

_____ *Trouble at the Bridge* (DK Readers: Lego). Dorling Kindersley, 2000.

Blackburn, Ken. *The World Record Paper Airplane Book*. Designs by Ken Blackburn and Jeff Lammers. Workman, 1994.

Blacklock, Dyan. *Olympia: Warrior Athletes of Ancient Greece*. Illustrated by David Kennett. Omnibus Books, 2000.

Block, Francesca. *Zine Scene: Do It Yourself Guide to Zines*. Girl Press, 1998.

Blum, Mark. *Galápagos in 3-D*. Chronicle, 2001.

Body: Bones, Muscle, Blood and Other Body Bits (Secret Worlds). Dorling Kindersley, 2001.

Bond, Peter. *DK Guide to Space*. Dorling Kindersley, 1999.

Bonson, Richard, and Richard Platt. *Disaster! Catastrophes That Shook the World*. Viking, 1997.

Bouchard, David. *The Journal of Etienne Mercier*. Illustrated by Gordon Miller. Orca, 1998.

Bowers, Vivien. *Crime Science*. Illustrated by Martha Newbigging. Owl, 1997.

_____ *Wow Canada! Exploring This Land from Coast to Coast to Coast*. Illustrated by Dan Hobbs and Dianne Eastman. Owl, 1999.

Brallier, Jess. *This Book Really Sucks!* Planet Dexter, 1999.

Branzei, Sylvia. *Grossology: The Science of Really Gross Things!* Addison-Wesley, 1995.

Bridges, Ruby, and Margo Lundell. *Through My Eyes*. Scholastic, 1999.

Brochu, Christopher, et al. *Dinosaurs* (The Time-Life Guides). Time-Life, 2000.

Brown, Gerry, and Michael Morrison, eds. *The 2001 ESPN Information Please Sports Almanac*. Hyperion, 2000.

Buckley, Jr., James. *Home Run Heroes: Big Mac, Sammy and Junior* (DK Readers, Level 3). Dorling Kindersley, 2001.

____ *Strikeout Kings* (DK Readers, Level 4). Dorling Kindersley, 2001.

Budd, Jackie. *Horses*. Kingfisher, 1995.

Bugs: A Close-up of the Insect World (Secret Worlds). Dorling Kindersley, 2001.

Bunting, Eve. *So Far from the Sea*. Illustrated by Chris K. Soentpiet. Clarion, 1998.

Burke, Judy. *Look What You Can Make with Paper Bags*. Boyds Mills, 1999.

Burton, A., Image Quest 3-D Staff. *3-D Reptile*. Dorling Kindersley, 1998.

Byam, Michele. *Arms and Armor* (Eyewitness). Stoddart, 1988/94.

Canadian Global Almanac. Macmillan Canada, 2000.

Cartwright, Fraser, and Jim Gilchrist. *The Living Atlas: All about Maps*. Gage, 1991.

Caslell, Maryanne. *Pioneer Girl*. Illustrated by Lindsay Grater. Tundra, 2001.

Cassidy, John. *Explorabook: A Kids Science Museum in a Book*. Klutz, 1991.

____ *The Klutz Book of Knots*. Klutz, 1985.

Cassidy, John, and Michael Stroud. *The Klutz Book of Magic*. Illustrated by H.B. Lewis and Sara Boore. Klutz, 1990.

Cheers, Gordon, and Julie Silk. *Killer Plants and How to Grow Them*. Puffin, 1996.

Chorlton, Windsor. *Woolly Mammoth: Life, Death and Rediscovery*. Scholastic, 2001.

Clarkin, Maura A. *National Gallery of Art Activity Book: 25 Adventures with Art*. Abrams, 1994.

Claybourne, Anna, et al. *The Usbourne Book of the Paranormal*. EDC Pub, 2000.

Cobb, Vicki. *Dirt and Grime*. Scholastic, 1998.

____ *Magic ... Naturally! Science Entertainments and Amusements*, rev. ed. Illustrated by Lionel Kalish. HarperCollins, 1993.

Coffey, Maria, with Debora Pearson. *My South Sea Adventure: Jungle Islands*. Photographs by Dag Goering. Annick, 2000.

Collins Essential Atlas of the World. HarperCollins, 1998.

The Cootie Catcher Book. Klutz, 1997.

Corbeil, Jean-Claude. *The Junior Visual Dictionary*. Scholastic, 1994.

____ *The Stoddart Visual Dictionary*. Stoddart, 1986.

Coster-Longman, Christina. *Creepy Crawlies* (Blow-Up! Junior Science). Illustrated by Ivan Stalio. Scholastic Canada, 2001.

Cowley, Joy. *Red-Eyed Tree Frog*. Photographs by Nic Bishop. Scholastic. 1999.

Cross, Robin. *Movie Magic*. Sterling, 1996.

Croswell, Ken. *See the Stars: Your First Guide to the Night Sky*. Boyds Mills, 2000.

Cruxton, Bradley J. *Discovering the Amazon Rainforest* (Discovery). Oxford, 1998.

Cushman, Karen. *Catherine Called Birdy*. Clarion, 1994.

_____ *Matilda Bone*. Clarion, 2000.

_____ *The Midwife's Apprentice*. Clarion, 1995.

Davies, Nicola. *Bat Loves the Night*. Illustrated by Sarah Fox-Davies. Candlewick, 2001.

Day, Trevor. *Ocean* (Popular Science Datafiles). Silver Dolphin, 2000.

Deary, Terry. *Horrible Histories: The Vicious Vikings*. Illustrated by Martin Brown. Scholastic, 1994.

De Kay, James T. *Meet Christopher Columbus* (Landmark Books). Illustrated by John Edens. Random House, 2001

Demi. *Gandhi*. McElderry, 2001.

Dewey, Jennifer Owings. *Poison Dart Frogs*. Boyds Mills, 1998.

Dewin, Ted. *Inside the Whale and Other Animals*. Illustrated with Steve Parker. Dorling Kindersley/Scholastic Canada, 1992.

Diehn, Gwen. *Making Books That Fly, Fold, Wrap, Hide, Pop Up, Twist and Turn*. Lark, 1998.

Dillon, Leo and Diane. *To Every Thing There Is a Season: Verses from Ecclesiastes*. Blue Sky/Scholastic, 1998.

Dinosaur (Eye Wonder). Dorling Kindersley, 2001.

Discovery Channel Insects and Spiders (An Explore Your World Handbook). Discovery Books, 2000.

Dixon, Norma. *Kites: Twelve Easy-to-Make High Fliers*. Illustrated by Linda Hendry. Morrow, 1996.

Dorling Kindersley Children's Atlas. Dorling Kindersley, 2000.

Dorling Kindersley Children's Illustrated Dictionary. Dorling Kindersley, 1994.

Dorling Kindersley Compact World Atlas. Dorling Kindersley, 2001.

Dorling Kindersley Concise Atlas of the World. Dorling Kindersley, 2001.

Duplacey, James. *Amazing Forwards*. Beechtree, 1996.

_____ *Champion NHL Defensemen*. Beech Tree, 1997.

_____ *Great Goalies* (NHL Hockey Superstars). Kids Can/Morrow, 1996.

_____ *Top Rookies* (NHL Hockey Superstars). Kids Can/Morrow, 1996.

Earle, Sylvia A. *Dive! My Adventures in the Deep Frontier*. National Geographic, 1999.

_____ *Hello, Fish! Visiting the Coral Reef*. Photographs by Wolcott Henry. National Geographic, 1999.

Edwards, Elwyn H. *Horse: A Visual Guide to Over 100 Horse Breeds from around the World* (Eyewitness). Stoddart/Dorling Kindersley, 1993.

Edwards, Yvonne, and Brenda Day. *Going for Kalta: Hunting for Sleepy Lizards at Yalata*. Jukurrpa Books, 1998.

Ellis, Sarah. *A Prairie as Wide as the Sea: The Immigrant Diary of Ivy Weatherall* (Dear Canada). Scholastic, 2001.

Erickson, Paul. *Daily Life in the Pilgrim Colony 1636*. Clarion, 2001.

Everts, Tammy, and Bobbie Kalman. *Horses*. Crabtree, 1995.

Facklam, Margery. *Spiders and Their Web Sites*. Illustrated by Alan Male. Little Brown, 2001.

Farndon, John. *Dictionary of the Earth*. Dorling Kindersley, 1994.

Farran, Christopher. *Animals to the Rescue! True Stories of Animal Heroes*. Illustrated by Warren Chang. HarperCollins, 2000.

Fison, Josie and Felicity. *Roald Dahl's Revolting Recipes*. Illustrated by Quentin Blake. Jonathan Cape, 1994.

Fogle, Bruce. *The New Encyclopedia of the Dog*. Photographs by Tracy Morgan. Firefly, 2000/DK, 2000.

Folder, Alan. *Paper Tricks*. Illustrated by Maureen Galvani. Tangerine Press, 2000.

Frank, John. *The Tomb of the Boy King*. Pictures by Tom Pohrt. Frances Foster/Farrar Straus Giroux, 2001.

Freymann, Saxton, and Joost Elffers. *How Are You Peeling? Foods with Moods*. Levine/Scholastic, 1999.

Froman, Nan. *What's That Bug? Everyday Insects and Their Really Cool Cousins*. Illustrated by Julian Mulock. Little Brown, 2001.

Funston, Sylvia. *Animal Feelings* (The Secret Life of Animals). Owl, 1998.

_____ *The Book of You. The Science of Why You Look, Feel and Act the Way You Do*. Illustrated by Susanna Denti. Photographs by Gilbert Duclos. Owl, 2000.

Ganeri, Anita. *The Oceans Atlas*. Illustrated by Lucian Corbella. Dorling Kindersley, 1994.

Geisert, Bonnie and Arthur. *Desert Town*. Houghton Mifflin, 2001.

_____ *Mountain Town*. Houghton Mifflin, 2000.

_____ *Prairie Town*. Houghton Mifflin, 1998.

_____ *River Town*. Houghton Mifflin, 1999.

Geographica's Family Atlas. Random House, Australia, 2000/Whitecap, 2001.

George, Jean Craighead. *How to Talk to Your Dog*. Illustrated by Sue Truesdell. HarperCollins, 2000.

Gerrard, Roy. *Wagons West!* Farrar, Straus & Giroux, 1996.

Gersten, Sheldon L., with Jacque Lynn Schaltz. *ASPCA Complete Guide to Dogs*. Chronicle, 1999.

Giblin, James Cross. *The Amazing Life of Benjamin Franklin*. Illustrated by Michael Dooling. Scholastic, 2000.

Golden, Christopher. *The 10-Minute Detective: 25 Scene-of-the-Crime Mystery Puzzles You Can Solve Yourself*. Prima, 1997.

Grace, Catherine O'Neill, and Margaret M. Bruchac. *1621 A New Look at Thanksgiving*. Photographs by Sisse Brimberg & Cotton Coulson. National Geographic, 2001.

Granfield, Linda. *In Flanders Fields*. Illustrated by Janet Wilson. Lester/Stoddart, 1995.

Gray, Samantha. *Ocean* (Eye Wonder). Dorling Kindersley, 2001.

Graydon, Don, and Kurt Hanson. *Mountaineering: The Freedom of the Hills*. 6th ed. The Mountaineers, 1997.

Greenaway, Theresa (Image Quest 3-D Staff). *Microlife*. Dorling Kindersley, 1998.

_____ *The Really Fearsome Blood-Loving Vampire Bat and Other Creatures with Strange Eating Habits*. Dorling Kindersley, 1996.

_____ *The Really Hairy Scary Spider and Other Creatures with Lots of Legs*. Photographs by Frank Greenaway and Kim Taylor. Dorling Kindersley, 1996.

_____ *The Really Wicked Droning Wasp and Other Things That Bite and Sting*. Stoddart, 1996.

Greenwood, Barbara. *Gold Rush Fever: A Story of the Klondike, 1898*. Illustrated by Heather Collins. Kid Can, 2001.

_____ *The Last Safe House: A Story of the Underground Railroad*. Illustrated by Heather Collins. Kids Can, 1998.

_____ *A Pioneer Thanksgiving: A Story of Harvest Celebrations in 1841*. Illustrated by Heather Collins. Kids Can, 1999.

Gregory, Kristina. *Cleopatra VII: Daughter of the Nile* (The Royal Diaries). Scholastic, 1999.

Guinness World Records 2002. Guinness World Records Ltd., 2001.

Hamilton-Barry, Joann. *Boldly Canadian: The Story of the RCMP*. Illustrated by Frances Clancy. Kids Can, 1999.

The Handy Science Answer Book, 2nd ed. Compiled by the Science and Technology Department of the Carnegie Library of Pittsburg. Visible Ink, 1997.

Hanrahan, Brendan. *Meet the Chicago Bulls*. Scholastic, 1996.

Hare, Tony. *Animal Fact File: Head-to-Head Profiles of More Than 90 Mammals*. Checkmark, 1999.

Harvey, Gil. *Ball Control* (Usborne Soccer School). Usborne, 1996.

Hawk, Tony, with Sean Mortimer. *Hawk. Occupation: Skateboarder*. ReganBooks/Harper Collins, 2001.

Hayhurst, Chris. *Snowboarding! Shred the Powder* (Extreme Sports). Rosen, 1999.

Haywood, Rosie. *The Great Dinosaur Search*. Usborne, 2001.

Hickman, Pamela. *Animals Eating: How Animals Chomp, Chew, Slurp and Swallow*. Illustrated by Pat Stephens. Kids Can, 2001.

_____ *Animals Senses: How Animals See, Hear, Taste, Smell and Feel*. Illustrated by Pat Stephens. Kids Can, 1998.

The History of Making Books (Voyages of Discovery). Scholastic, 1995.

Hodge, Deborah. *Beavers, Deer, Moose, Elk and Caribou*. Illustrated by Pat Stephens. Kids Can, 1998.

_____ *The Kids Book of Canada's Railway and How the CPR Was Built*. Kids Can, 2000.

Hooper, Meredith. *Antarctic Adventure: Exploring the Frozen South* (DK Readers, Level 4). Dorling Kindersley, 2000.

Hopping, Lorrain Jean. *Lightning!* (Will Weather, Level 4). Scholastic, 1999.

Imes, Rick. *Incredible Bugs: An Eye-Opening Guide to the Amazing World of Insects*. Macmillan Canada, 1997.

Jackson, Donna. *The Bone Detectives: How Forensic Anthropologists Solve Crimes and Uncover Mysteries of the Dead*. Photographs by Charlie Fellenbaum. Little Brown, 1996.

Jackson, Ellen. *The Book of Slime*. Illustrated by Jan Davey Ellis. Millbrook, 1997.

Jenkins, Steve. *Slap, Squeak and Scatter: How Animals Communicate*. Houghton Mifflin, 2001.

Jennings, Gael. *Bloody Moments: Highlights from the Astonishing History of Medicine*. Illustrated by Roland Harvey. Annick, 2000.

Johnson, Neil. *Photography Guide for Kids*. National Geographic, 2001.

Johnstone, Michael. *The History News in Space*. Candlewick, 1999.

Julivert, Marias Angels. *The Fascinating World of Bats*. Illustrated by Marcel Stocias Studios. Barron's, 1994.

Kalman, Bobbie, and Heather Levigne. *What Is a Bat?* (The Science of Living Things). Crabtree, 1999.

Katz, Alan. *Take Me Out of the Bathtub and Other Silly Dilly Songs*. Illustrated by David Catrow. McElderry, 2001.

Keiran, Monique. *Albertosaurus: Death of a Predator* (Discoveries in Palaeontology). Raincoast, 1999.

Kelley, James. *Baseball* (Eyewitness). Dorling Kindersley, 2000.

Kelly, Sarah. *Amazing Mosaics*. Barron's, 2000.

Kent, Peter. *Hidden under the Ground: The World beneath Your Feet*. Scholastic, 1998.

KidsCooking: A Very Slightly Messy Manual. Illustrated by Jim M'Guinness. Klutz, 1987.

King, Andy. *Mountain Biking* (Play by Play). Lerner, 2001.

Kirshner, David. S. *Reptiles and Amphibians* (My First Pocket Guide). National Geographic, 1996/2001.

Kisseloff, Jeff. *Who Is Baseball's Greatest Hitter?* Henry Holt, 2001.

Knight, Tim. *Journey into the Rainforest*. Photographs by Juan Pablo Moreiras and Tim Knight. Oxford, 2001.

Knotts, Bob. *Martial Arts* (A True Book). Children's Press/Grolier, 2000.

Kramer, Stephen. *Hidden Worlds: Looking through a Scientist's Microscope*. Photographs by Dennis Kunkel. Houghton Mifflin, 2001.

Kroeger, Mary Kay, and Louise Borden. *Paperboy*. Illustrated by Ted Lewin. Clarion, 1996.

Lacey, Sue. *Start with Art: Animals*. Copper Beech, 1999.

_____ *Start with Art: People*. Copper Beech, 1999.

Lambert, David. *DK Guide to Dinosaurs: A Thrilling Journey through Prehistoric Times*. Dorling Kindersley, 2000.

Langley, Andrew. *Castle at War: The Story of a Siege*. Illustrated by Peter Dennis. Dorling Kindersley, 1998/Stoddart, 1999.

____ *Renaissance* (Eyewitness). Stoddart/Dorling Kindersley, 1999.

Lasky, Kathryn. *Elizabeth I: Red Rose of the House of Tudor* (The Royal Diaries). Scholastic, 1999.

Latimer, Jonathan, and Karen Nolting. *Songbirds* (Peterson Field Guides for Young Naturalists). Illustrated by Roger Tory Peterson. Houghton Mifflin, 2000.

Lauber, Patricia. *The True-or-False Book of Cats*. National Geographic Society, 1998.

____ *What You Never Knew about Tubs, Toilets and Showers*. Illustrated by John Manders. Simon & Schuster, 2001.

Layden, Joe. *Meet the Los Angeles Lakers*. Scholastic, 1997.

Lessem, Don. *Inside the Amazing Amazon*. Illustrated by Michael Rothman. Crown, 1995.

Levithan, David. *In the Heart of the Quake* (Disaster Zone Books). Scholastic, 1998.

Levy, Elizabeth. *Awesome Ancient Ancestors!* (America's Horrible Histories). Illustrated by Daniel McFeeley. Scholastic, 2001.

____ *Who Are You Calling a Woolly Mammoth?* (America's Horrible Histories). Illustrated by Daniel McFeeley. Scholastic, 2001.

Linton, Marilyn. *Just Desserts and Other Treats for Kids to Make*. Kids Can, 1998.

Little, Jean. *Orphan at My Door: The Home Child Diary of Victoria Cope*. Scholastic, 2001.

Llewellyn, Claire. *The Best Book of Bugs*. Kingfisher, 1998.

Lourie, Peter. *The Mystery of the Maya: Uncovering the Lost City of Palenque*. Boyds Mills, 2001.

Macaulay, David. *Building Big*. Walter Lorraine/Houghton Mifflin, 2000.

____ *Building the Book Cathedral*. Houghton Mifflin, 1999.

____ *Castle*. Houghton Mifflin, 1977.

____ *Cathedral: The Story of Its Construction*. Houghton Mifflin, 1973.

____ *The Way Things Work*. Houghton Mifflin, 1988.

Macdonald, Fiona. *Mummies and Tombs* (Discovery). Lorenz, 2000.

Mackin, Bob. *Soccer: The Winning Way*. Greystone/Douglas & McIntyre, 2001.

MacLeod, Elizabeth. *Alexander Graham Bell: An Inventive Life*. Kids Can, 1999.

____ *Get Started Stamp Collecting for Canadian Kids*. Kids Can, 1996.

____ *Lucy Maud Montgomery: A Writer's Life*. Kids Can, 2001.

Macy, Sue. *Bull's Eye: A Photobiography of Annie Oakley*. National Geographic, 2001.

Madgwick, Wendy. *Questions and Answers: Dinosaurs*. Kingfisher, 2000.

Maestro, Betsy. *Bats: Night Fliers*. Illustrated by Giulio Maestro. Scholastic, 1994.

Manson, Ainslie. *House Calls: The True Story of a Pioneer Doctor*. Illustrated by Mary Jane Gerber. Groundwood, 2001.

Markle, Sandra. *Pioneering Ocean Depths*. Atheneum, 1995.

Mason, Adrienne. *Mealworms: Raise Them, Watch Them, See Them Change*. Illustrated by Angela Vaculik. Kids Can, 1998.

Mattison, Chris. *Snake*. Dorling Kindersley/Firefly, 1999.

Maynard, Christopher. *Informania: Sharks*. Candlewick, 1997.

McFarlane, Brian. *Hockey for Kids: Heroes, Tips and Facts*. Kids Can, 1994.

McMillan, Bruce. *Wild Flamingos*. Houghton Mifflin, 1997.

McWhirter, Norris. *Norris McWhirter's Book of Historical Records*. Virgin, 2000.

Meikle, Marg. *Funny You Should Ask: Weird but True Answers to 115 ½ Wacky Questions*. Illustrated by Tina Holdcroft. Scholastic Canada, 1998.

_____ *You Asked for It! Strange but True Answers To 99 Wacky Questions*. Illustrated by Tina Holdcroft. Scholastic Canada, 2000.

Meyer, Carolyn. *Anastasia: The Last Grand Duchess* (The Royal Diaries). Scholastic, 2000.

_____ *Mary, Bloody Mary* (Young Royals). Gulliver/Harcourt, 1999.

Michael, David. *Step-by-Step Making Kites*. Illustrated by Jim Robins. Kingfisher, 1993.

Mitton, Jacqueline. *Aliens: The Facts behind the Fiction* (Informania). Candlewick, 2000.

Montgomery, Sy. *The Man-Eating Tigers of Sundarbans*. Photographs by Eleanor Briggs. Houghton Mifflin, 2001.

_____ *The Snake Scientist*. Photographs by Nic Bishop. Houghton Mifflin, 1999.

Morse, Jenifer Corr. *Scholastic Book of World Records 2002*. Scholastic, 2001.

Morton, Alexandra. *In the Company of Whales: From the Diary of a Whale Watcher*. Orca, 1993.

Mummies and the Secrets of Ancient Egypt (Secret Worlds). Dorling Kindersley, 2001.

Munro, Margaret. T*he Story of Life on Earth*. Illustrated by Karen Reczuch. Groundwood, 2000.

Murawski, Darlyne A. *Bug Faces*. National Geographic, 2000.

Murphy, Jim. *The Great Fire*. Scholastic, 1995.

Nature Lab: The Ultimate Nature Pack. Advantage, 2000.

Newson, Lesley. *The Atlas of the World's Worst Natural Disasters*. Viking, 1998.

NHL Best Shots. Dorling Kindersley, 2001.

Nicholson, John. *The First Fleet: A New Beginning in an Old Land*. Little Ark/Allen & Unwin, 1995.

_____ *Fishing for Islands: Traditional Boats and Seafarers of the Pacific*. Allen & Unwin, 1999.

_____ *A Home among Gum Trees: The Story of Australian Houses*. Little Ark/Allen & Unwin, 1997.

Nicolson, Cynthia Pratt. *Comets, Asteroids and Meteorites* (Starting with Space). Illustrated by Bill Slavin. Kids Can, 1999.

____ *Mysterious You Baa! The Most Interesting Book You'll Ever Read about Genes and Cloning.* Illustrated by Rose Cowles. Kids Can, 2001.

____ *Volcano!* Kids Can, 2001.

Nilsen, Anna. *Art Fraud Detective.* Kingfisher, 2000.

O 'Brien, Lisa. *Lights, Camera, Action! Making Movies and TV from the Inside Out.* Illustrated by Stephen MacEachern. Owl, 1998.

Oppel, Kenneth. *Silverwing.* Simon & Schuster, 1997.

Orr, Richard. *The Burrow Book.* Dorling Kindersley, 1997.

____ *Nature Cross-Sections.* Dorling Kindersley/Scholastic Canada, 1995.

Osborne, Will, and Mary Pope. *Knights and Castles: A Nonfiction Companion to the Knights at Dawn* (Magic Tree House Research Guide #2). Illustrated by Sal Murdocca. Random House, 2000.

Oxford Children's Encyclopedia of Our World. Oxford University, 1999.

Oxford Children's Encyclopedia of Science and Technology. Oxford University, 1999.

The Oxford Encyclopedia World Atlas. 3rd ed. Oxford University, 2000.

The Oxford Junior Atlas. 3rd ed. Oxford University, 1996.

Parker, Steve. *The Body Atlas.* Illustrated by Giuliano Fornari. Dorling Kindersley, 1993.

____ *Medicine* (Eyewitness). Dorling Kindersley, 2000.

Pellant, Chris. *Rocks and Minerals.* Dorling Kindersley, 2000.

Pinchuik, Amy. *Make Amazing Toy and Game Gadgets* (Popular Mechanics for Kids). HarperCollins/Greey de Pencier, 2001.

____ *Make Cool Gadgets for Your Room* (Popular Mechanics for Kids). HarperCollins/Greey de Pencier, 2001.

Piven, Joshua, and David Borgenicht. *The Worst-Case Scenario Survival Handbook.* Chronicle, 1999.

Platt, Richard. *Castle Diary: The Journal of Tobias Burgess, Page.* Transcribed by Richard Platt. Illuminated by Chris Riddell. Candlewick, 1999.

____ *The Coolest Cross-Sections Ever.* Illustrated by Stephen Biesty. Dorling Kindersley, 2001.

____ *Extreme Sports* (DK Readers, Level 3). Dorling Kindersley, 2001.

____ *Spy.* Dorling Kindersley, 2000.

____ *Stephen Biesty's Cross-Sections: Castle.* Illustrated by Stephen Biesty. Dorling Kindersley/Scholastic Canada, 1994.

____ *Stephen Biesty's Incredible Body: Meet the Teams That Make the Body Work!* Scholastic Canada/Dorling Kindersley, 1998.

____ *Stephen Biesty's Incredible Explosions: Exploded Views of Astonishing Things.* Illustrated by Stephen Biesty. Dorling Kindersley/ Scholastic Canada, 1996.

____ *Technology and Communications* (Datafiles series). Silver Dolphin, 2000.

Preller, James. *The NBA Book of Big and Little.* Scholastic, 1998.

Prelutsky, Jack. *Dragons Are Singing Tonight*. Illustrated by Peter Sis. Greenwillow, 1993.

Pringle, Laurence. *An Extraordinary Life: The Story of a Monarch Butterfly*. Paintings by Bob Marstall. Orchard, 1997.

____ *Sharks! Strange and Wonderful*. Illustrated by Meryl Henderson. Boyds Mills, 2001.

Pritchard, Louise. *My Pony*. Stoddart/Dorling Kindersley, 1998.

Pulleyn, Micah, and Sarah Bracken. *Kids in the Kitchen: 100 Delicious, Fun and Healthy Recipes to Cook and Bake*. Sterling, 1995.

Rain Forest (Eye Wonder). Dorling Kindersley, 2001.

Raskin, Lawrie, with Debora Pearson. *My Sahara Adventure: 52 Days by Camel*. Photographs by Lawrie Raskin. Annick, 1998.

Reynolds, David West. *Star Wars: Incredible Cross-Sections*. Illustrated by Hans Jenssen and Richard Chasemore. Dorling Kindersley/Stoddart, 1998.

____ *Star Wars: The Visual Dictionary*. Stoddart/Dorling Kindersley, 1998.

Richard, Jon, ed. *World Championship Wrestling: The Ultimate Guide*. Dorling Kindersley, 2000.

Ripley, Catherine. *Why Is Soap So Slippery? And Other Bathtime Questions*. Illustrated by Scot Ritchie. Owl, 1995.

Roberts, Jeremy. *Rock and Ice Climbing! Top the Tower* (Extreme Sports). Rosen, 2000.

Roberts, Jerry. *The Amazing Book of Paper Boats*. Illustrations and paper engineering by Willy Bulock. Chronicle Books, 2001.

Robson, Graham. *The Illustrated Dictionary of Classic Cars*. MBI/Salamander, 2001.

Rogers, Kirsteen, et al. *The Usborne Internet-Linked Science Encyclopedia with 1,000 Recommended Web Sites*. Usborne, 2000.

Rossiter, Sean. *Goal Scoring*. Douglas & McIntyre, 1997.

Royston, Angela. *Space Station: Accident on Mir* (DK Readers, Level 4). Dorling Kindersley, 2000.

Salvi, Francesco. *The Impressionists: The Origins of Modern Painting* (Masters of Art). Illustrated by L.R. Galkante and Andrea Ricciardi. Peter Bedrick, 2000.

Sandler, Martin W. *Civil War* (A Library of Congress Book). HarperCollins, 1996.

Sayre, April Pulley. *Dig Wait Listen: A Desert Toad's Tale*. Illustrated by Barbara Bash. Greenwillow, 2001.

Scamander, Newt. *Fantastic Beasts and Where to Find Them*. Arthur Levine/Scholastic, 2001.

Schlegel, Elfi, and Claire Ross Dunn. *The Gymnastic Book: A Young Person's Guide to Gymnastics*. Key Porter, 2000.

Schlesinger, Willy and Max. *Scooter Mania!* St. Martin's Griffin, 2000.

Schmidt, Norman. *Best Ever Paper Airplanes*. Sterling, 1995.

Scholastic Atlas of the World. Scholastic, 2001.

Scott, Tim. *History Hoaxes*. Illustrated by Scoular Anderson. Hodder, 2000.

Sheikh-Miller, Jonathan. *Sharks* (Usborne Discovery). Usborne, 2000.

Shemie, Bonnie. *Building Canada*. Tundra, 2001.

Sida, Geoff. *Electronics Lab: The Ultimate Electronics Pack*. Silver Dolphin, 2000.

Simon, Seymour. *Animals Nobody Loves*. Sea Star, 2001.

____ *Destination: Jupiter*. HarperCollins, 1998.

____ *Gorillas*. HarperCollins, 2000.

____ *Now You See It, Now You Don't: The Amazing World of Optical Illusions*, rev. ed. Drawings by Constance Ftera. Beech Tree/Morrow, 1998.

____ *Sharks*. HarperCollins, 1995.

____ *Tornadoes*. HarperCollins, 1999.

Sis, Peter. *Starry Messenger: A Book Depicting the Life of a Famous Scientist, Mathematician, Astronomer, Philosopher and Physicist, Galileo Galilei*. Frances Foster/FSG, 1996.

Skreslet, Laurie, with Elizabeth MacLeod. *To the Top of Everest*. Kids Can, 2001.

Smyth, Ian. *The Young Baseball Player: A Young Enthusiast's Guide to Baseball*. Stoddart/Dorling Kindersley, 1998.

Solheim, James. *It's Disgusting and We Ate It! True Food Facts from around the World—and throughout History*. Illustrated by Eric Brace. Simon & Schuster, 1998/Aladdin, 2001.

Somerville, Louisa. *Look Inside Cross-Sections: Rescue Vehicles*. Illustrated by Hans Jenssen. Dorling Kindersley, 1995.

Space. (Eyewitness). Dorling Kindersley, 2001.

Spalding, Andrea and David. *The Lost Sketch: Unlock the Mystery Found in the Boxcar* (Adventure.Net). Whitecap, 1999.

Squashing Flowers Squeezing Leaves: A Nature Press and Book. Klutz, 2001.

Stanford, Quentin H. *Canadian Oxford World Atlas*. Oxford University Press, 1998.

Stanley, Diane. *Leonardo da Vinci*. Morrow, 1996.

Stanley, Jerry. *Hurry Freedom: African Americans in Gold Rush California*. Crown, 2000.

Steele, Philip. *The Best Book of Mummies*. Kingfisher, 1998.

____ *Castles*. Kingfisher, 1995.

Stephens, Rebecca. *Everest* (Eyewitness). *Dorling Kindersley, 2001.*

Stevens, Beth Dvergsten. *Colorful Kites*. Perfection Learning, 2000.

Stoops, Erik D. and Sherrie. *Sharks*. Sterling, 1995.

Sturges, Philemon. *Bridges Are to Cross*. Illustrated by Giles Laroche. Putnam, 1998.

Sukach, Jim. *Clever Quicksolve Whodunit Puzzles: Mini-Mysteries for You to Solve*. Illustrated by Lucy Corvino. Sterling, 1999.

Suzuki, David, and Kathy Vanderlinden. *Eco-Fun: Great Projects, Experiments and Games for a Greener Earth*. Kids Can, 2001.

Swanson, Diane. *Animals Eat the Weirdest Things*. Illustrated by Terry Smith. Whitecap, 1998.

_____ *Burp? The Most Interesting Book You'll Ever Read about Eating.* Illustrated by Rose Cowles. Kids Can, 2001.

_____ *Coyotes in the Crosswalk: Canadian Wildlife in the City.* Illustrated by Douglas Penhale. Whitecap, 1994.

_____ *Feet That Suck and Feed* (Up Close). Illustrations by Rose Cowles. Greystone, 2001.

_____ *Head Gear That Hides and Plays* (Up Close). Illustrations by Rose Cowles. Greystone, 2001.

_____ *Hmm? The Most Interesting Book You'll Ever Read about Memory.* Illustrated by Rose Cowles. Kids Can, 2001.

_____ *Nibbling on Einstein's Brain: The Good, the Bad and the Bogus in Science.* Illustrated by Warren Clark. Annick, 2001.

_____ *Skin That Slimes and Scares* (Up Close). Illustrations by Rose Cowles. Greystone, 2001.

Swinburne, Stephen R. *Bobcat: North America's Cat.* Boyds Mills, 2001.

Tames, Richard. *Knights and Battles* (Discovery Plus). Silver Dolphin, 2001.

Tanaka, Shelley. *The Buried City of Pompeii: What It Was Like When Vesuvius Exploded.* Illustrated by Greg Ruhl. Scholastic/Madison, 1997.

_____ *Discover the Iceman.* Illustrated by Laurie McGaw. Hyperion/Madison, 1997.

_____ *Graveyards of the Dinosaurs.* Illustrated by Alan Barnard. Scholastic/Madison, 1998.

_____ *In the Time of Knights.* Illustrated by Greg Ruhl. Hyperion/Madison, 2000.

_____ *On Board the Titanic.* Illustrated by Ken Marschall. Scholastic Canada/Madison; Hyperion/Madison, 1997.

_____ *Secrets of the Mummies: Uncovering the Bodies of Ancient Egyptians.* Illustrated by Greg Ruhl. Hyperion/Madison, 1999.

Taylor, Barbara. *Elephants* (Nature Watch). Lorenz, 1999.

_____Taylor, Barbara. *Great Apes* (Nature Watch). Lorenz, 2001.

_____Taylor, Barbara. *Spiders* (Nature Watch). Lorenz, 1999.

Thayer, Ernest Lawrence. *Casey at the Bat.* Illustrated by Christopher Bing. Handprint, 2000.

Tookoome, Simon, with Sheldon Oberman. *The Shaman's Nephew: A Life in the Far North.* Stoddart, 1999.

Tornadoes and Other Dramatic Weather Systems (Secret Worlds). Dorling Kindersley, 2001.

Trotman, Felicity. *Living in Space.* Barron's, 1999.

The Truly Tasteless Scratch and Sniff Book. Dorling Kindersley, 2000.

Turnbull, Andy, with Debora Pearson. *By Truck to the North.* Annick. 1999.

The Ultimate Lego Book. Dorling Kindersley, 1999.

Ultimate Robot Kit. Dorling Kindersley, 2001.

The Visual Dictionary of Cars (Eyewitness Visual Dictionaries). Dorling Kindersley, 1992.

Visual Encyclopedia of Animals. Dorling Kindersley, 2001.

Walker, Niki, and Sarah Dann. *Soccer in Action* (Sports in Action). Crabtree, 2000.

Walker, Richard. *3-D Human Body*. Dorling Kindersley, 1999.

____ *The Children's Atlas of the Human Body: Actual Size Bones, Muscles and Organs in Full Color*. Milbrook, 1994.

____ *DK Guide to the Human Body: A Photographic Journey through the Human Body*. Dorling Kindersley, 2001.

Weekes, Don. *Explosive Hockey Trivia*. Greystone, 2001.

____ *Extreme Hockey Trivia*. Greystone, 1999.

____ *Rockin' Hockey Trivia*. Greystone, 2000.

Whatley, Bruce, and Rosie Smith. *Whatley's Quest*. Illustrated by Bruce Whatley. Angus & Robertson/HarperCollins, 1994.

Wheatley, Nadia. *My Place*. Illustrated by Donna Rawlins. HarperCollins, Australia, 1988.

White, E.B. *Stuart Little*. Illustrated by Garth Williams. HarperCollins, 1945.

Whiteley, Opal. *Only Opal: The Diary of a Young Girl*. Illustrated by Barbara Cooney. Paperstar, 1997.

Wick, Walter. *A Drop of Water: A Book of Science and Wonder*. Scholastic, 1997.

Wilkes, Angela. *A Farm through Time: The History of a Farm from Medieval Time to the Present Day*. Illustrated by Eric Thomas. Dorling Kindersley, 2001.

Williams, Brian. *Forts and Castles*. Viking, 1994.

Williams, Marcia. *Fabulous Monsters*. Candlewick, 1999.

Willis, Paul M. *Rocks and Minerals* (My First Pocket Guide). National Geographic, 1997/2001.

Wilson, Ian and Susan. *The Gold Rush*. Gordon Soules, 2001.

Wilson, Stacy. *The Hockey Book for Girls*. Kids Can, 2000.

Winston, Mary, ed. *American Heart Association Kids' Cookbook*. Illustrated by Joan Holub. Times/Random House, 1993.

Wistow, David, and Kelly McKinley. *Meet the Group of Seven* (The Art Gallery of Ontario). Kids Can, 1999.

Withrow, Sarah. *Bat Summer*. Groundwood, 1999.

The World Almanac and Book of Facts 2002. World Almanac, 2001.

The World Almanac for Kids 2002. World Almanac, 2001.

World Atlas for Young Explorers. National Geographic, 1998.

Wulffson, Don L. *The Kid Who Invented the Trampoline: More Surprising Stories about Inventions*. Dutton, 2001.

Yolen, Jane. *Sacred Places*. Illustrated by David Shannon. Harcourt, 1996.

Yorke, Jane, ed. *The Big Book of Trains: The Biggest, Fastest, Longest Locomotives on Rails*. Scholastic Canada/Dorling Kindersley, 1998.

Young, Jay. *The Art of Science: A Pop-Up Adventure in Art*. Candlewick, 1999.

Zelinsky, Paul O. *Rapunzel*. Dutton, 1997.

Znamierowski, Alfred. *The World Encyclopedia of Flags*. Lorenz, 1999.

Index

Credits

Every effort has been made to acknowledge all sources of material used in this book. The publisher would be grateful if any errors or omissions were pointed out, so that they may be corrected.

Arnold, Caroline; Cross Giblin, James; Pringle, Laurence; Ride, Sally; Simon, Seymour—excerpts from *Popular Nonfiction Authors for Children: A Biographical and Thematic Guide* by Flora R. Wyatt, Margaret Coggins and Jane Hunter Imber. Copyright 1998 Libraries Unlimited. Reprinted by permission of Libraries Unlimited— (800) 237-6124 or www.lu.com.

Carter, Betty and Richard Abrahamson—excerpt from "Castles to Colin Powell: The Truth about Nonfiction" in *Into Focus: Understanding and Creating Middle School Readers* by K. Beers and B. Samuels, eds. Copyright 1998. Reprinted by permission of Christopher-Gordon.

Cashan, Asher—excerpt from "Who Teaches the Child to Read" in *New Horizons in Reading* by J. Merritt, ed. Copyright 1976. Reprinted by permission of the International Reading Association.

Cassady, Judith—excerpt from "Wordless Books: No Risk Tools for Inclusive Middle-Grade Classrooms" in *Journal of Adolescent & Adult Literacy,* 41, 6. Copyright 1998. Reprinted by permission of the International Reading Association.

Caswell, Linda and Nell Duke—excerpt from "Non-Narrative as a Catalyst for Literacy Development" in *Language Arts,* 75, 2. Copyright 1998. Reprinted by permission of the National Council of Teachers of English.

Crook, Marion—excerpts from speaking engagements. Reprinted by permission of Marion Crook.

Fink, Rosalie—excerpts from "Successful Dyslexics: A Constructivist Study of Passionate Interest Reading" in *Journal of Adolescent & Adult Literacy,* 39, 4. Copyright 1995. Reprinted by permission of the International Reading Association.

Freedman, Russell; Fritz, Jean—excerpts from *Using Nonfiction Trade Books in the Elementary Classroom: From Ants to Zeppelins* by Evelyn Freeman and Diane Person, eds. Copyright 1992. Reprinted by permission of the National Council of Teachers of English.

Graves, Donald—excerpts from *Investigate Nonfiction* by Donald Graves. Copyright 1989. Reprinted by permission of Heinemann, Portsmouth, NH.

Guthrie, John and Ann McCann—excerpt from "Characteristics of Classrooms That Promote Motivations and Strategies for Learning" in *Reading Engagement: Motivating Readers through Integrated Instruction* by J. Guthrie and A. Wigfield, eds. Copyright 1997. Reprinted by permission of the International Reading Association.

McCormick Sandra—excerpt from *Instructing Students Who Have Literacy Problems:* 3/E by McCormick. Copyright 1999. Reprinted by permission of Pearson Education, Inc., Upper Saddle River, NJ.

McKenna, Michael, et al.—excerpt from "The Electronic Transformation of Literacy and Its Implications for the Struggling Reader" in *Reading & Writing Quarterly,* 15, 2. Copyright 1999. Reprinted by permission of Taylor & Francis Ltd.

Pilkey, Dav—excerpt from the Web site www.pilkey.com. Reprinted by permission of Dav Pilkey.

Robb, Laura—excerpt from "Helping Reluctant Readers Discover Books" in *Book Links,* March. Copyright 1998. Reprinted by permission of *Book Links.*

Routman, Regie—excerpts from *Conversations: Strategies for Teaching, Learning and Evaluating* by Regie Routman. Copyright 2000. Reprinted by permission of Heinemann, Portsmouth, NH.

Skretta, John—excerpt from "King's Works and the At-Risk Student" in *Reading Stephen King* by Brenda M. Power, Jeffrey Wilhelm and Kelly Chandler, eds. Copyright 1997. Reprinted by permission of the National Council of Teachers of English.

Truscott, Diane, et al.—excerpt from "Poor Readers Don't Image, or Do They?" in *Reading Research Report,* No. 38. Copyright 1995. Reprinted by permission of co-author Barbara Walker.

Worthy, Jo, et al.—excerpt from "What Johnny Likes to Read Is Hard to Find in School" in *Reading Research Quarterly,* 34, 1. Copyright 1999. Reprinted by permission of the International Reading Association.